LIVE Your Sunshine

Be Your Light

Working with Conscious Thought to Feel Good

Lesley MacCulloch

BALBOA.
PRESS
A DIVISION OF HAY HOUSE

Balboa Press books may be ordered through booksellers or by contacting:

Balboa Press
A Division of Hay House
1663 Liberty Drive
Bloomington, IN 47403
www.balboapress.com
1 (877) 407-4847

Because of the dynamic nature of the Internet, any web addresses or links contained in this book may have changed since publication and may no longer be valid. The views expressed in this work are solely those of the author and do not necessarily reflect the views of the publisher, and the publisher hereby disclaims any responsibility for them.

The author of this book does not dispense medical advice or prescribe the use of any technique as a form of treatment for physical, emotional, or medical problems without the advice of a physician, either directly or indirectly. The intent of the author is only to offer information of a general nature to help you in your quest for emotional and spiritual well-being. In the event you use any of the information in this book for yourself, which is your constitutional right, the author and the publisher assume no responsibility for your actions.

Any people depicted in stock imagery provided by Thinkstock are models, and such images are being used for illustrative purposes only. Certain stock imagery © Thinkstock.

Print information available on the last page.

ISBN: 978-1-5043-8204-5 (sc)
ISBN: 978-1-5043-8206-9 (hc)
ISBN: 978-1-5043-8205-2 (e)

Library of Congress Control Number: 2017909315

Balboa Press rev. date: 07/06/2017

This book is for everyone:

It matters not who or what you are, just
that you are open and committed
and ready to believe that you *can*.

For

You

Because you *are* and you *can*.

We do not see things as they are,
we see things as we are.

—Anaïs Nin

Contents

Introduction xv

Living Your Sunshine.. xvii

Your Adventure xxi

Change.. xxiii

My Aim for You xxiv

Feel – That's You Talking xxvi

The Structure of This Book xxix

My Reason for Using the Word Adventure xxxi

What Have I Got To Do With It? xxxii

My Easter 2016 Epiphany............................. xxxv

Part One
What's True

What's True 1

Our Universe 3

You Are Connected to Something Huge.......................... 4

Tapping Into the Energy.. 9

You Are Energy..10

Chakras and Chakra Blocks 15

We All Have Free Will 23

The Choice is Yours 25

Decisions, Decisions 27

For You or For Them 30

Benefiting from the Law of Attraction 33
What You Focus On 36
Being Grateful..40
Building Appreciation into Your Day 43
Thank Someone in Writing...47
Taking Advantage of Momentum 49
Allow Yourself to Receive 51

Love and Fear 54
Choose Not to Fear 57
Getting Along With Your Ego 60
You Have Been Taught to Live in Fear 63
The Amygdala: Fear Centre of the Brain.......................63
Love: Live it, Love it, Be it 67
Listen to the Message in the Fear, and Feel the Love 68

Spirituality versus Religion...74
God..75
Religion 77
You're a Spiritual Being..78

Part Two
What Else is True?

What Else is True?...83
You Are and You Can 84

You Are 88
You Are Perfect..92
You Are Beautiful 96
You Are Human..99
You Are Love 104
You Are You 109

Are You Your Values? Are Your Values You?.................. 113

You Are the Light 119

You Can 121

You Can Open Up 126
You Can Accept 134
Accept by Releasing, Detaching, and Letting Go 135
What if You Can't Accept... 136
You Can Become Curious.. 143
You Can Think Big, High, and Wide 148
Chat With You 150
You Can Be Grateful.. 154

You Can Intend 156
It's All About You – Not Them 160
You Can Visualise 164
You Can Feel 167
Conscious Thoughts Can Change Your Feelings 170
First Things First 170
Throughout the Day 174
Acknowledge the Message in the Fear; Consciously
Share Only Love 179
Focus on Three Things You Love 181
Acknowledge the Fear 181

You Can Receive 187
You Can Breathe 190
The Deep Breathing Process Explained 193
You Can Believe 197
The Importance of Positive Belief 198
It's All in the Attitude.. 200
You Can Let Go... 205
What's Not Essential to Your Life? (Be Honest)............ 208

You Can Allow 211

    Meditate 213

    Be 219

You Can Live Spiritually 222

You Can Feel 222

Time With You 231

Back to Your Senses 234

    Pay Attention 237

    See and Look At 239

    Listen and Hear 240

    Taste and Smell 247

You Can Connect With Nature 249

You Can Move 254

You Can Be True to You 258

Resolutions – New Year, New Month, New Day 260

Live Your Sunshine, Be Your Light 264

Where to Now 267

Thank You to My Guides 269

Books on My Shelf Today 271

References 283

About the Author 289

*I*ntroduction

THANK YOU. THANK YOU FOR BEING here. Thank you from me – and thank you from *you* – for opening your heart, your mind, and your self to the possibility – to the *fact* – that you *can* feel better.

Your new mantra from hereon in is just that: **can**. You can, you *can*, you *CAN!*

Feel that. Feel it. Feel what 'can' feels like. *Can* is such a wide-open word. It opens everything up and it makes you want to stretch your arms out to the sky and the sun, to the amazingness of our world, our planet, our universe. 'Can' brings possibility. 'Can' helps you to *believe*. 'Can' reminds you that you're capable, strong, powerful, and empowered. 'Can' is your resource, your tool, your friend. 'Can' is with you everywhere you go.

'Can' helped me bring this book to you – and that's the truth.

You *can* feel better, and you *will* if you're ready to step back into your power, step back into your life. You *will* if you're open and ready to take the lead, take ownership, and take responsibility of *you*. You *will* if you're ready to commit to trying some of the suggestions offered to you as we progress through this book. Keep in touch whenever you feel you need to for extra support, guidance, and help from someone who believes in you.

♥ You can, you *can*, you *CAN!*

For years you've been living a double life. There's the *you* you were born to be – beautiful, loving, compassionate, confident, kind, and full of self-esteem, patience, and truth. Then there's your ego, your head (or head *ache*) – the one who goes on constantly, caring too much about what others think, the one who puts you – and others – down, the one who judges and criticises you – and others – the one who tells you you're inferior, no good, useless, hopeless, selfish. Your ego tells you to worry, to feel guilty, embarrassed, worthless, to play games. Your ego tells you that you have to win, and it even makes decisions for you.

But only because you let it.

Just focussing on writing these few lines made my heart sink.

I want to tell you something: You are a powerful and empowered being. You've got everything to offer. You've got so much inside you, and you *can* feel good more often than you do. As we stroll through this book forming a new relationship with each other, I'm going to help you to take back your power, your choices, your decisions, and your life. I'm going to help you understand why some things work well for you and other things don't – and to change the things that don't. By working together, we'll help you to draw out more of the beauty, the confidence, the love, and the truth of who you are inside.

Who you are inside is who you were born to be: you – the happy, easy-going, confident person you were before the big arms of society got their claws into your ego and taught you fear.

Together we're going to help you find your inner spirit and unearth your truth, your inner strength, your shining light. Together we're going to help you bring more feelings of joy, hope, peace, harmony, trust, love, and acceptance into your life.

Together we're going to help you to look and listen *inside*, instead of everywhere else, for your answers, your guidance, your decisions.

You're a beautiful person, and you've made the first big step to changing your life and feeling good by being right here right now.

I am your friend, your inspirer, and your companion. I am on this journey with you. You are not, and will not be, alone. This book is for you, to you, and all about you.

♥ Know you're not alone.

Living Your Sunshine

This isn't just a reading book; it's a doodle, scribble, and create book. This is a book that's going to encourage you to *feel* your life and *create* your life. If these are two new concepts to you, then really do be prepared to step outside your comfort zone; really do be prepared to try different things. This may take a lot of courage. Reading and *doing* this book may take you to places you've never been before, to thoughts you've never allowed yourself to consider before. I'll be right there with you.

We're brought up to judge and to make decisions about things we've never even tried. We're quick to put down, belittle, or offend – or take offence – if something doesn't quite fit within our realm of acceptability. Do you like the side of you that does that? Throughout *Live Your Sunshine – Be Your Light* I encourage you to question those sorts of traits within yourself. I encourage you to really look at and nail down why you do some of what you do, why you feel the need to say some of what you say. This questioning alone will help you to uncover a lot about yourself. You'll find yourself with no good reasonable answer a lot of the time; hence, if you're quite serious about living a more feel-good life, you'll pay attention to the things you're doing, saying, and allowing to enter your energy field.

Words alone don't teach us life's lessons. Words alone don't enable us to live true to ourselves or to unwrap our authenticity and shining light. Words can give us information and suggestions, but it's only from our openness and willingness; our participation; our effort; our application of tips, ideas, and suggestions to our own reality; our conscious commitment to trying new things for size that we learn and then begin to apply appropriate changes to our lives – changes that actually work for us.

That's why there's space for your doodles, scribbles, and creations throughout this book. I encourage you to really let your creative side out. Let your thoughts flow naturally and easily. Let your mind zone out, let your creativity soar, and let yourself *feel*. Let your truth shout out, let your true self sing, and I will sing with you. The whole reason for this book is to offer you support, inspiration, and somewhere to start. Draw, write, scribble, doodle – do what you like on the pages. It's not about being an artist; it's about creating and flowing. It's about allowing yourself the time to dig deep – and a bit deeper – to find, create, and *be* the colour in your life. Changing the habits and beliefs of a lifetime can be overwhelming, and doesn't happen overnight. It can feel easier to stay the same rather than trying to work out what to tackle first. This book is your trusted guide and mentor; it is here to encourage you, challenge you to think differently and seek inside, and to help unearth the leader inside you. The content comes from a lifetime of noticing and paying attention to how I was feeling, processing that information, and then making changes to ensure I was mostly feeling nice feelings – feeling 'ease'. Sometimes the process of making a change, while hard, is easier than living with the consequences of not making the change or having the same things happen over and over again.

While there are no rules about how you approach or use the information in this book, I've written it in a particular order, and it does flow from start to finish. Some of what comes later refers to ideas I've presented earlier. I'd definitely suggest working through it in order, from beginning to end.

I would also love it if you did the following:

- Get yourself some coloured pencils so you can really doodle, scribble, and create. Colour your life and free your spirit.
- If you're a bigger doodler, scribbler, and creator than these pages allow (which part of me hopes you are), get yourself a separate doodling, scribbling, and creating pad or book so you can go for broke. That's what I'd have to do. This is about you letting go and flowing, not 'looking good'. Leave behind *can't* and embrace *can*.
- If you're daunted by the doodle, scribble, and create concept, please just try it. Sometimes you can doodle a number or a symbol or a letter, and with free mind and free hand it can lead to places and realisations you'd never have imagined. Allow yourself the opportunity for self-exploration. Letting go with the colour in your hand can be meditative, calming, and quite revelatory.
- Be prepared to allow yourself to properly listen to and acknowledge your heart, your intuition, your truth.
- Grant yourself at least an hour – if not longer – each time you sit down to work through this book. As you create, your mind will open up, and you'll recognise what it *feels* like to you let *you* out. Allow that momentum. Don't try to work through the book too quickly; there's a lot in it. Better to give it a bit longer once or twice a week than a quick snippet every day. Give it a chance to resonate and be absorbed into

your light inside because initially it'll reach only your head. You need to *feel* this book.

- Spend a lot of your time opening your mind, feeling, doodling, scribbling, creating, drawing, writing, singing – and ultimately savouring the space to realise what's actually happening in various areas of your life and what you can do to change some of it.

- Sit quietly enjoying the space and the silence, and breathe deeply for a few minutes before getting started again each time you come back. Give yourself time to mentally leave what you were doing behind, and get back into your *you* and your 'I can' space. The momentum of the day takes hold of all of us. It might take you a good few minutes after you've sat down quietly to actually bring yourself back to the creative, conscious-thinking, and light-focused headspace you want to be in as you work your way through the book and nurture *you*. If you can't 'do' silence yet, focus on the sounds of nature or play some properly calming, relaxing, concentration, de-stressing music softly.

Soul Coaching® – *28 Days to Discover Your Authentic Self* is a book by Denise Linn that promotes cleansing and clearing of the mental, emotional, physical, and spiritual aspects of life in the form of a four-week program. When I was working through the book, I actually planned the evenings, afternoons, and sections of time that I would sit down to read through that day's information and carry out its thought-provoking, life-changing exercises. I treated the program like a course of study, I suppose, and I blocked time out on my calendar. If you're committed to changing, feeling better and stepping up, consider committing to a schedule so that you have clear, uninterrupted space to focus on your life.

♥ Colour your life and free your spirit.

Your Adventure

We're all on our own adventure, you included. Part of your adventure is to grow, create, and become, once again, *you*. And wouldn't it be nice if you were enjoying your adventure a little bit more?

We're not here to attempt to change who you are. That's not what this is about. We're here to look at changing the balance. Currently, you're always looking and listening *outside* for answers; we're going to turn that around and encourage you to look and listen *inside*. The happier, freer, feel-good you is in there – always has been there. And from time to time you've listened to, acknowledged, and acted on that *you*. Mostly, though, you've buried that you – your true self – deep down inside as you've been brought up to meet the expectations, judgments, and perceptions of others, and reacted to the circumstances of your life. You've been conditioned to allow yourself to be guided by your ego, and your ego only feeds you fear.

Changing the balance doesn't mean having to make great big changes, or any one major change that'll turn your whole life around. But it does mean consciously reviewing what's going on in your life, paying attention to how you're allowing it to affect you, and then doing something about it.

That's right – pay attention to *how you're allowing it to affect you*. Don't blame it for what *it's* doing to you. You're going to pay attention to how events and people are making you feel and then do something about those feelings by taking back your own power, asserting your discipline, and becoming more conscious of your reactions and your thoughts.

Ultimately, we're going to help you feel more liberated and able to be yourself, to accept being yourself, and to be confident being yourself. We're going to ward off *ego-you* and let *true-you* sing from the rooftops.

Some of the exercises may feel a bit scary. That's okay. The exercises are intended to encourage you out of your place of comfort; they're intended to stretch your thinking, help you to learn more about yourself, and get back in touch with the true and honourable inner *you*.

This is your adventure, and you'll be the one deciding what changes you make. Nobody else. Nobody else needs to even know you're reviewing some aspects of your life. However, do be prepared to step outside your comfort zone. Staying inside your comfort zone – staying where life is safe and where you feel protected (but not necessarily particularly great) – isn't the way you're going to change anything. Indeed, it is the way to ensure you live with permanent doubt, worry, fear, monotony, sadness, and guilt as your friends, or, rather, your very heavy backpack. It is also the way to ensure you're likely to have regrets at some stage in your life.

💜 This is *your* adventure.

You can step outside your comfort zone in small but significant ways that are personal to you and that nobody else notices, so don't think you need to be making public displays of all or even any of the changes you're going to be making for yourself.

By the same token, there may be people, circumstances, and networks in your life that you realise (you've probably known for a long time) aren't good for you. As you work through your review of various aspects of your life, you may find you naturally take steps to move away from the ones that aren't serving you, or change the part they play in your life.

💜 Step outside your comfort zone.

You're committing here to making changes for *you*. This may be the first time in a long time that you've done something for you, so congratulations! This could be the best decision you've made in years. If you take on even some of what's in this book, or if some of what's in this book leads to other positive changes in your life, you'll feel different. And if you embrace the difference any small change can make, you'll gradually be on a change-making roll, and you'll feel empowered, energised, and very much better inside.

Change

Don't be afraid of this word. Embrace it. Change will come into your life whether you like it or not, so why not be the one to take the lead and make changes of your choice – of your very own crafting? Often it feels safer to stay where we are. The old saying 'better the devil you know (than the devil you don't)' can have us stuck in a rut for our whole lives, doing everything we don't like with or for people we don't particularly enjoy being with. If you're here now, and you're not feeling great, then why wouldn't you grab the opportunity to try some things that could help you feel better? Especially if you know you're supported and have people on your side!

I know the answer: making changes might mean bringing some form of conflict, fear, or judgment into your life. Well, so be it. You've got conflict, fear, and judgment already, so what changes? Accept that, in order to be true to yourself and believe genuinely and strongly in yourself, you might just need to stop meeting the expectations of others and actually start chatting with and listening to *you* for a change. Get to know yourself now. Think of your true self – your inner authentic self – as your best and unconditionally loving friend, and think of your ego as that niggling ton weight of annoyance that sits at the back of your head somewhere, tripping you up, stopping you, casting aspersions, insults, and offences at you all day long. Ego-head tells you he's helping you out, but believe me, he's not helping. Thank him and let him know you can look after yourself.

That's a brief discussion on change when in some worlds people are making a living through change theories, curves, and methodologies, and managing changes in workplaces. Don't make change bigger than it needs to be. The weather changes; you're used to it. The seasons change; you're used to it. Your children change as they grow up. Your friends change. You change your clothes, you change your house, you change your job, your holiday destination, your hair ... What? You haven't changed your hair in years? Go on then! Change your hair! Essentially, nothing stays the same, so why should you and your thoughts, beliefs, opinions, actions, and behaviours have to stay the same for your whole life? Why should everything else get to change and evolve and you don't?

Embrace it. Welcome change, and take it slowly and at your own pace. This is about you and only you.

And remember, you're not alone.

♥ Change is an opportunity not to be missed.

My Aim for You

I want you to feel better. I want everybody to feel better. I want the world to feel better. I feel sad at the thought of so many people feeling so demoralised and defeated, guilty, full of worry and woe. People are nervous, down, and out of love with themselves. They feel that they need to *keep up* in one way or another as they remain focused on all that is bleak. I want us all to sing our songs, to notice the wonder around us, and to feel amazing.

We spend our lives focusing on and allowing ourselves to be affected by many things we can't change. We can't change the weather, we can't change the wars (at least not single-handedly), we can't change the news, we can't change the football score, we can't change the hunger, and we can't change what others do, think, or say. These are all external factors that just are. But we can look inside at our reactions to all of these things. Is it really healthy, worthwhile, or useful to spend so much energy on external things we can't do a thing about? That doesn't mean we shouldn't be empathetic, generous, loving, and giving to charities and others. Indeed, genuine giving (and not just of money but of *you*), caring, kindness, and compassion are what eventually will change the world. But it does mean that there's no point living these external factors as if they're yours to own or change. It's better to focus on doing things to make yourself feel better because then you'll make others feel better, and maybe one day the domino effect that's just getting started will capture the whole world in its loving embrace.

By looking inside, your outlook, approach, and attitude will change, and when you feel better, you make others feel better. That is the only way we can hope to have an impact on any of these conditions and events.

So, with that in mind, I'm here to play my own little part in serving our world. Rather than focusing on conditions and events I can't change, I'm focusing on you, because I know I can help you. I know I can offer you hope, guidance, encouragement, and choices you've forgotten were yours to make.

I want us all to reach out to the sky, and know we can! My aim for you is that you will feel better and live your life for *you*. You can achieve this by doing the following:

- Address the imbalance you've got going on in your life.
- Change from predominantly thinking to predominantly feeling; from predominantly negative, cynical, angry, anxious worrying to predominantly positive, optimistic, loving, creative, accepting.

- Become more conscious of when you're feeling bad or thinking negatively so you can consider the message and do something about it.
- Become more assertive and empowered over what you're doing, thinking, saying, feeling, and how you're behaving – instead of simply reacting.
- Proactively intend the way you want your day to be and feel.
- Forgive yourself, accept yourself, and let go of all judgment.
- Try out behaviours that could ultimately have a life-changing effect on how you feel.
- Become your own leader.
- Open your ears and your heart.
- Own your own power.
- Reclaim your life, your decisions, your actions, your focus, and get to the root of who you really are.
- Listen to *you*, and no longer let your ego, fears, friends, family, society, the media, and excuses run your life.
- Take responsibility – own your life and everything that's in it.
- Do things that will help you *feel* far healthier and much more energised.

Life really isn't about winning or losing. We spend too much time comparing ourselves and thinking we need to keep up with something or somebody, or both. Life is about having fun, feeling ease, and being part of an adventure, and we've forgotten how to enjoy that adventure as our blinkers have blocked our view.

♥ Step into your power — do it for *you*.

Feel – That's You Talking

Everything you need in order to be able to find good feelings is already inside you. But to begin with, tread cautiously and patiently. Your ego has been running the show and leading the way since you were a toddler. It's how we're brought up in Western society:

to believe that everything external matters, including the way we look, and to stop listening to what is inside us. Our ego guides us to conform to what society expects of us, or what it has been accustomed to *believe* society expects of us. We've been conditioned to live by our ego since we were pre-school age and had to start growing up and 'fitting in'. The ego is the part of us that kicks in to stop us doing or saying things that our true self wants us to do or say. I wouldn't be publishing this book if I listened to my ego. Our souls – our true selves – were crushed as rules, regulations, expectations, comparisons, and doubt took hold, and we were slotted into conformity.

But they weren't destroyed. *You* are strong. Your little light still shines, and you *can* be yourself. You're a bright, shining being and you're about to give more oxygen to that light. And with every small step forward, that light will emerge more and more and you will notice your confidence, strength and belief in yourself flourish.

The main way to feed your light is to *feel* your way forward. Feelings are *you* talking to you, guiding you, helping you make decisions that are right for you. Only after you've started to become conscious of your feelings can you determine whether they feel good, bad, or somewhere in between; what they're related to; or why they're occurring. And only then can you change them if they need changing.

As we progress through the book, we'll look at how you determine whether a feeling is coming from *you* – from within – or whether it's a feeling being generated as a result of you listening to your ego. Here's an easy and very basic way to think about this: if it's a good feeling, it's *you;* if it's not a good feeling, it's usually something that's coming from your head. Those are the feelings we're going to call messages. We're not going to discount your ego altogether. We grow the most from our most challenging, often our most negative experiences, so your ego does have an important part to play as a messenger. We're going to pay attention to the feelings that are coming from what's going on in your head, and we're going to take steps to address those feelings so that they either disappear or become good feelings. You are an empowered, assertive human being, and you deserve to shine! *You* choose how much air space the messages from your ego messenger may be granted as well as how you deal with those messages.

Our inner beings and intuition do send us feelings of discomfort too. Once you tune into your heart space, you'll be able to tell the difference between the guidance coming from deep within, and the messages coming from your head.

I propose that will you find, by the end of working your way through this book, that you have changed inwardly. You will look the same, but better. Inwardly you will feel like a new person, and you will want to know what's next for you on your adventure. My hope is that you will describe the transforming you in the following ways:

- I feel less tense.
- I feel softer.
- I care much less about my outward appearance and the opinions of others.
- I am singing inside!
- I experience much more joy from what's around me.
- I no longer feel stagnant, flat, or numb inside or as if someone's dropped rocks in my stomach.
- I feel more alive, less stressed, more accepting, and less bothered by people and things that irk me during my day – or used to irk me.
- I believe in myself.
- I forgive me.
- I honour my self and my uniqueness.
- I recognise and accept my own power and the place I deserve on this earth.
- I feel responsible, accountable, capable, and empowered.

- I know I am worthy, deserving, and valuable.
- I choose to pursue good feelings and sunshine.
- I follow my inner guidance, and I embrace the messages being delivered through my fear.
- I want to keep learning, absorbing, and feeling around for more.
- I know what to do to find all of the above when I'm having a bad day. I am patient and know that it takes time.

♥ Do it for yourself – you deserve it.

The Structure of This Book

I had various thoughts on how to structure the book, and ultimately the one I've used came to me during quiet time with my colouring pencils and my scribbling pad. Part One serves as the context and presents a view of the world as we know it, but a view we often ignore or disbelieve. I felt the content of Part One was important to share with you to help you understand where I am coming from and to help you gain the most benefit from the exercises throughout.

Part One contains the information that helped me to make sense of everything. I've had numerous 'wow' moments over the years when I've read or heard something that rings so true that it explains loudly and clearly so much about what 'is' and what I've experienced in my life to that date. Hence the first part of *Live Your Sunshine – Be Your Light* is my offering to you, my version of what's out there and what I believe to be true. It is also what quantum science and researchers are proving and finding out more and more about every single day. By giving you that information as your foundation, my intention is to provide some answers for you, and maybe fill in some gaps and establish a solid stepping stone from which you can launch forward in your venture to live your sunshine.

I want you to have the benefit of knowing the information in Part One before you get seriously down to creating whatever opportunities in your life you'd like to create, and whatever changes in your life you choose to make. It's the bits we're not told about in the mainstream news, or at school, or by our religions. We're taught science, but we're not taught to expect or to remember that science evolves and is ever changing as it continues to find out new things. That's what science *is*, so we can't expect that what we were taught in school or university won't be – and maybe even has already been – superseded or changed by now by new revelations. There's a lot happening in quantum physics at the moment that isn't being shared in mainstream media. Evolution isn't something that happened before our time. Evolution is something that's always happening, and that we're a part of. We can't keep ignoring new revelations.

So, Part One contains the bits I've pieced together myself, like a jigsaw really – a bit here and a bit there as I've travelled along my own adventure creating ways to feel good. In my early stages of writing, I realised that, finally, I could see a whole that I could articulate to others.

The 'facts' we've trusted for 300 years to explain the universe and our role in it are flawed. They're based on two assumptions that have been proven false:

False Assumption 1
The space between 'things' is empty.

False Assumption 2
Our inner experiences of feeling and belief have no effect on the world beyond our bodies.[1]
Gregg Braden

Part Two is all about you. You *are* and you *can*. You *are* perfection, truth, and beauty, and you *can* choose to open up, set intentions, receive, live spiritually, and be true to *you*. You are beholden to no one and nothing. I want for you to bloom, to enjoy, and to expand throughout Part Two. I want you to spread your wings and really fly in Part Two.

Throughout the book are various exercises and activities, all of which I'd like you to answer creatively – not necessarily with too much thought, but with plenty of feeling. These are the doodle, scribble, create pages I mentioned earlier. The doodle, scribble, and create exercises are what the book is about and are what will guide you through your changes. The exercises are about challenging yourself, challenging your beliefs, trying new things. Take this chance to experiment with new thoughts and ideas. I'm not here to tell you what you should or shouldn't believe or what you should or shouldn't think. Only you can decide that. I'm here to offer openings and ideas that you will benefit from if you allow yourself the opportunity to do so, and that will help you to listen to your inner self instead of the world around you and what's in your head.

To offer some realistic examples, I've included a lot of what's worked for me over the years. If I were your personal guide and we were working together in person, I would help you to identify relevant examples from within your own life. There will be plenty of occasions when you've listened to your heart and shone your light, and when things have gone right and you've felt great. As we are working at a distance, so to speak, I feel that some of my own examples might help you with context and understanding. My own experiences may help you more easily see where I'm coming from. And this might help you apply some appropriate changes to your own life.

My Reason for Using the Word Adventure

Just one final thing: I was originally going to talk about your spiritual 'journey', but I felt the word *journey* to be a little bit bland. A journey, to me, is simply the process of getting from one place to the next. I don't consider myself as being on a journey; neither do I consider you as being on a journey. I believe we're all on an adventure. And by that I don't mean we're all climbing mountains in the Himalayas or kayaking the Amazon. I simply mean that life is our creation. It is our opportunity, and it can be our joy. It provides us with moments of uncertainty and risk; it throws us curveballs, challenges, and opportunities to stretch ourselves; and it gives us magical moments of excitement, peace, and true connection to everything around us.

Add some spice to your journey, and make it an adventure.

♥ Create the rest of your life — starting now.

What Have I Got To Do With It?

Okay, this is the part where I share a bit about me for those who either are interested, or are looking for relevance or credentials from this unheard-of woman who's writing books on living your light. How does she know I've got a light – and what on earth does she mean by that anyway? How does she know I 'can'? What's she done that's so great and makes her think she can help me colour my grey life?

If you don't care about any of that, then just skip this bit and keep going to Part One.

The answer to the first question is – if I've got a light, you've got a light. Stick with it, and you'll find out.

To the second question I say – I know you can because I believe in you. And I know that, deep down, you *can* and *you want to*. So let's do it together. Join me and sing, live, and shine, earth star!

The answer to the third question is – nothing special. I have done nothing special to gain the information and experience I need to be able to help you. I've done nothing other than live my life. I've not been to a Buddhist retreat in India or on a shamanic journey to Peru; neither have I been suicidal or close to death. I have not healed myself from cancer, a brain tumour, or a spinal injury. I'm just an average, honest, hard-working, self- and socially-aware observer of life, the universe, and everything around me. I'm still on my own creative adventure, and I'm learning every single day. I have simply been living my life and trying to find ways of living it that make it feel nicer, easier, better, and more enjoyable.

If something doesn't feel good or right, I look for – I create – ways to make it feel better, or I change it or my reaction to it. I do something about it. I accept that I can't and shouldn't need or want to change anything other than myself. I listen to what my 'gut' is telling me; I listen to my inner guidance, my intuition, my heart. I listen to how I *feel*.

I don't enjoy feeling sick in my stomach or having a sore head or feeling a heavy weight on my shoulders. I don't enjoy taking what people say personally when it's not meant that way, or feeling overly sensitive, precious, or judged. I don't like feeling angry, guilty, flat, numb, embarrassed, critical or criticised, exhausted, drained, or worried. I don't enjoy feeling that life's too hard.

Of course, just like you, I do feel these things. I am human. I have grown up and have been living in the same world you live in, conditioned by the same global events, news, education, religions, communities, bureaucracies, and hierarchies. But my commitment to myself has been and continues to be that I want to feel these negative things as little as possible. Negative feelings hold me up, they burden me, they drag me down, they don't help me to achieve, and they don't make me nice company. So when I feel them, I listen to them, and then I work out why I'm feeling them.

By doing that, I remain empowered. I take responsibility. I am the leader of me, and I do whatever I need to do to rid myself of these sorts of feelings and generate nicer ones.

And that doesn't mean sticking my head in the sand about the source of any of these issues. It means doing what needs to be done, within the realms of staying true to myself, and without upsetting anyone.

But that doesn't mean people don't get upset.

In order to live true to myself, I have to allow myself to accept that I have responsibility for me, and that others have responsibility for themselves. I must allow myself to accept that others are living their own truths, which, if they really were, would mean we could all speak freely without feeling judged, criticised, condemned, battered, bullied, and as if we're upsetting someone – or whatever it is we decide we're going to feel when we communicate as we always should have done.

I must allow myself to accept that others will react to me in whatever way their egos or their true inner selves guide them to react. I don't ever set out to insult anybody or do anybody an injustice, so if anyone is insulted or offended by me, then I must accept that for what it is. I cannot go changing my views, or my messages – my truth – or the way I'm saying things just in case someone is insulted, because the next person may not be insulted. Where would it ever end? I do, however, try to speak from my heart with love, objectivity, compassion, empathy, constructive truths, and lightness, and I forgive, forget, and hold no grudges.

I try not to pander to people's dismay about their lives, but to help inspire them with hope, encouragement, and truth along with ways they can stop taking things that are being said to them the wrong way, or looking too far into things for messages and judgements that aren't there. I try to open them to ways they can graciously accept the lives, views and opinions of others, and get on with all that is theirs.

My Easter 2016 Epiphany

For a while I wondered what was next for me. Indeed, I remember writing to Meadow Linn after I'd finished my coaching adventure through her mum's amazing *Soul Coaching®* book and saying that I was curious to know 'what was next'. That book – and my own commitment to Denise Linn's series of coaching exercises inside the book – had a very big impact on my life.

For an even longer time, I've known that my strengths are in guidance and leadership, focussing heavily on assisting individuals in their own personal and life development. I totally love helping others to feel inspired, enabled, creative, encouraged, motivated, capable, independent, competent, empowered, supported, confident, strong, and full of hope. I love encouraging people to believe that they absolutely *can* do things they've never felt – for whatever reason – they should or could. All too often we don't do or say things because we have decided in our minds – our egos have told us – that we either can't or we'd 'better not', for no good reason whatsoever.

For about six months I kept getting a picture of myself in my mind that related to the upcoming Easter weekend in 2016. There was nothing in the picture that showed me it was Easter; I just knew it was. I had a grin on my face, I was holding my hands to the sun as if I was cheering, and I had a strong sense that something was going to happen over that weekend.

And it did. During some beautiful and very grounding quiet time over the weekend while I was just being, I got a very clear message – a very clear realisation that it was time for me to turn a corner. It was time for me to share with others what I'd been doing for myself all my life. It was time to share my ways with the world in the form of a coaching or a guide book.

I've created plenty of training materials and accredited qualifications over the years, but I didn't ever think I'd be sitting here writing a book. In fact, I've discounted suggestions from people over the years that I should write a book, having never felt remotely interested or inclined to do so. Indeed, I have found myself quite in awe of people who could maintain the level of attention, detail, and focus required to create a book. That's why it was with complete amazement that I found myself receiving from the depths within me the message – the *knowing* – that I was to write a book.

So here we are. And it feels like the most right thing in the world. That's what happens when you quiet your mind, open up, and listen to *you*. You really do hear what you're saying, know you *can*, and live your light.

♥ Quiet your mind; *you* have the answers.

PART ONE

What's True

What's True

I BELIEVE IN YOU, THAT'S WHAT'S true. That's the number one reason why I'm here.

But what's true of your world?

As I have mentioned, the first part of *Live Your Sunshine – Be Your Light* focuses on what is known and true of the world you are living in. This is information I wasn't aware of in my early ventures into improving my approach to my life and how I let things make me feel. But over the past ten to fifteen years I've read and learned a lot, and the facts about our world are continually evolving as scientists find out more and more.

So, although I wasn't aware of a lot of the points I share in Part One during the earlier stages of my own spiritual enrichment journey, I feel they are important for you to understand as you review where you're at in your life and consider where you want to be. I would definitely have made progress, and experienced insight and awakening, a little more quickly if I'd known and understood how much more I could influence my life, and what I had inside me that would help me reach higher and burst into flower.

I also like to know why and how. I'm curious, inquisitive, and interested, so I spend a lot of time looking for answers and information. I thought it might help you if I shared some of that information. Part

One contains a lot of the answers – the current known truths – about our universe, which, in turn, highlights how incredibly difficult we've made life for ourselves.

But it also highlights how we can use what's around us and what we know to make life so much easier. Awareness is empowering, and knowing and realising means we can take a step back and work with what we now know *is*.

💜 Believe in *you* – I do.

Our Universe

YOU MAY OR MAY NOT BE aware of (or you may have chosen to ignore or dismiss as many have), some of what's going on around us in this big world and what's going on in that vastness, that space around us.

We are all tiny parts of an expansive universe – sometimes now being called the quantum field or realm, other times known as source, God, or the cosmos.

The universe is varying levels of vibrational energy that contain everything we are and know.

> Therefore the whole Universe is actually made out of energy, and what we perceive as matter is also energy. The collective energy waves of the Universe, which might be referred to as 'invisible moving forces', comprise the field …[2]
>
> Bruce Lipton

There are laws that operate within that expanse of energy. We've grown up knowing some of these laws, such as the one that creates gravity, but most of them have been kept under wraps.

We are energy too, a vibrational part of that expanse of energy called the universe. There is energy inside our physical bodies and surrounding our bodies. The energy surrounding our physical bodies is known as an aura. The energy beyond our auras expands into that huge quantum field of energy.

♥ You are energy.

You Are Connected to Something Huge

This way of thinking may be a little different to what you are used to. It may be a bit challenging. You may not like it, but it's important to follow your progress through this book in the context of this information. In fact, without acceptance or understanding of the fact that you're a tiny piece of energy – a very important and connected tiny piece – in something that's far bigger than your own little world or even the big world we live in, you'll lose a lot of benefit and value from the greater broader learning you'll derive from working through these chapters. That energy – that vibration, these laws – works *with* you to create your reality. What's 'happening to you' isn't just accidental. When you realise and understand this even just a little bit, you can then use it to your advantage and make your world just a little bit easier and more enjoyable.

Have a think about times when you've just *known* you need to do something, or when you've received a strong and powerful message from somewhere inside you that you can't quite explain. Perhaps you felt that you needed to be somewhere, or that something was just right (or not right). What do you think was happening there?

Think about times when you've 'felt a vibe' or had a strong inner sense about something.

This is the universe working with your inner being. This is your true self, your heart, your intuition. This is all of these things that are one, that are *you*, connecting with the higher energy that's all around you and guiding you along your way. If you can picture something like that happening – an invisible connection, or telephone line, between you inside and the tops of the trees and beyond – then you'll be able to see yourself operating perfectly without any needless interruptions or negative self-talk from your head. Hold on to that picture!

You are so much more than just your mind and your body. This sort of internal communication is happening all the time, but most of the time we don't listen to it because we're too busy listening instead to our egos, our logic, our reason, our friends.

Think also of times when you have walked into a room and felt an atmosphere. What else, other than energy, other than something bigger than anything you can touch, could that be?

You have been connecting and connected with universal energy your whole life. So, accept that fact here and now because this knowing will help you to pay attention to more of what's right for you and what's in front of you.

This is also about you building the confidence not only to listen to *you*, but to stop listening to others who are guiding you along the path *they* want you on (which they may be doing consciously or subconsciously). The path others would rather see you on is often quite a different path to the one you know, deep down, you'd rather be on. This is about you no longer conforming and no longer striving to meet expectations of other people – or your imagined expectations of other people. It is about standing up for yourself and having faith and belief in yourself and the messages you're receiving from your heart. The messages you receive from deep inside are your highest thoughts, your intuition, and they're coming from your connection to universal energy. They're the best guidance for you at any point in time. They are your highest vibration, and they are pure love. Don't go looking for alternatives, disputes, negotiations, or 'ways out'; I want you to trust yourself. As you open yourself to your own guidance, and follow your own guidance, you will continue to receive more guidance, so don't be afraid to do what your true self is asking you to do.

💜 *You are already connected to a perfect support system.*

There are lots of reasons – or excuses – that encourage us to close ourselves off to information and facts and other ideas we don't want to hear. But the simple fact is, there's something going on around you that's very much bigger than you – and me, and your family members and friends, your religion, your government, your culture, and your social network. As a society we generally choose to ignore this big 'something' or condemn it because it's 'weird'. It's easier to do that than it is to be laughed at, or than it is to take the time to understand how universal energy and its laws work and can be used to our own benefit.

It's easier just to believe everything we were brought up to believe by those we've touched and who have touched us, than it is to venture into even just listening to something else – another perspective, new discoveries in science – so we might become more informed and actually make up our own minds about the way we'd like to be and live our lives. For many of us it's become easier to live closed off than it is to even try opening our hearts and minds. We make excuses, rendering everything on the horizon at fault for whatever's going on in our lives, instead of standing tall, taking responsibility for our lives and leading our own way.

We tend to sneer or scoff at people who believe there's something more, something much bigger than just their own little domain. We don't even want to actually take a look at what it is they know or are doing, and how they're managing to live a life that's calm and relaxed, peaceful and contented.

Of course, part of the difficulty is that we can't 'see' the energy. We tend not to believe what we can't see: I'll believe it when I see it. Yet there's a lot of truth in the reverse of that philosophy: I expect that when I believe it, I'll see it.

Think 'open', 'believe', 'trust', 'love', 'attract' and 'feel'. I urge you to start *feeling* more, and then to pay more attention to what your feelings are telling you.

♥ Feel it, believe it, and you'll see it.

Open your mind to new thoughts and ideas. Toy around with the fact that you are energy inside and that you're surrounded by an invisible energy, your aura. Contemplate the fact that there is a lot more of that energy above, around, and beyond the realms of your body. When you open up and even just entertain the fact that you're part of something so much bigger, the little things – the difficult people, the hiccups in your plans – matter less, and often even stop mattering at all. The weight lifts a little as you realise that the energy around you is your unconditional friend, and it can help you, guide you, and work with you better than the sources of support you currently rely on – media, friends, family members, society, colleagues, your ego.

In fact, your whole perception changes. You are no longer annoyed by things that annoy you now because you see them differently and in true perspective. You are able to see – and live and love! – the brighter, lighter side of life because you're connecting with *you*, and *you*, by default, operate in connection with that bigger, higher universal energy.

Don't be put off, and don't be scared if this is all a bit too much. You don't have to 'get it' yet; this is just foundation information that will help you. As you look back on it, as you work through the exercises in this book, it'll make sense. Take your time and force nothing. Just go gently, and be open to receive and try.

♥ Open up to something bigger, and life will get easier.

Doodle, Scribble, Create!

Reflect, in colour and creation, on what you've just been reading. Read the 'You Are Connected to Something Huge' section again. Research the ideas yourself. Consider what, if any of it, you've heard before. What does it mean to you? If it's confronting, why is it confronting? Is your mind fighting it? Does it feel right? What feels right about it?

These are just guiding questions. You don't need to spend too long here, but do take some time to allow what you've just read to settle, and to get used to being receptive to different information and different ways of thinking.

Open up and challenge your 'norm'! Doodle, scribble, create and feel, in colour, your way through the exercise.

Tapping Into the Energy

Sit quietly and rub the palms of your hands together fairly quickly for a few moments – enough to warm them up. Slowly move them apart. What can you feel? Close your eyes.

Move your hands further apart and then closer together without touching. Move them further apart again. Feel the invisible extending and contracting ball, the fuzzy air, the pulsating of your hands. Whatever you want to call it, this is energy. Within a few seconds, you've moved, generated, and connected with some of the energy that's around you.

In early 2003, raging bushfires shot uncontrollably through a vast area of national park near Brooklyn on the Hawkesbury River in New South Wales, Australia. A matter of weeks after the last of the fires had been extinguished, I was driving north, out of Sydney, along the freeway that ran through this region.

Words will never portray what my senses experienced that day. As I drove round a bend, I came face-to-face with a breath-taking sight. Thousands of bright green new shoots had formed on the tips of scorched, charcoal-scarred trees, over an expanse that stretched to the horizon and totally contradicted the powerful stench of the still-burning cinders that was reaching my nostrils. On a normally fairly uninspiring drive home along the freeway, I encountered something that arrested my senses like never before. It was one of the most humbling, moving, awesome sights I had ever seen. Tears ran down my face. I was covered in goose pimples and completely in the grasp of the regeneration I saw before me.

The traffic and human life around me paled into total insignificance, and the sheer massive presence, the absolute and overwhelming natural beauty and *power* in those trees humbled me instantly.

Nothing can describe what came over me, and the respect I felt, in those few moments that day as I came around that corner and faced that commanding energy and true power of life. The contradiction between the amazing bright green example of youth and the black charcoal span of devastation stretching as far as the eye could see (and the nose could smell) was testament to the strength of life, wellness, and health. It was evidence that life can't be pulled out from under us quite as easily as we might think. We are those trees. We are that energy, that resilience. We can do that too. We can stand tall, we can be strong, we can be knocked down and come back stronger.

That those trees had that incredible and amazing power, that Mother Nature could do that, taught me more about energy and life and power in about thirty seconds than reading any book could ever have done.

❤ Power, resilience, strength = *you.*

You Are Energy

I urge you and encourage you not just to go with the words in this book, but to really take a holistic approach to what you're reading. Include your whole being. Sense the energy in and around you and zone in on your feelings. Experiment. Try things. Given the right attention, your feelings will energise you. Your feelings will help you to find the strength to open up to new thoughts, to open up to try new things. Your feelings will help you to open up to new possibilities, to the truth of what *is* in the world. Your feelings will help you to step over the fear, out of your comfort zone, and into the experience of trying something new.

The words alone don't teach you anything. The feelings, the energy, the experiences, and the emotions are your guides. Even as I was just sitting here trying to describe that day, feeling it again and reliving it from the other side of the world over thirteen years later, I had to stop and just be with it for a few minutes. Energy is powerful, grounding, inspiring, and deeply humbling. Just allowing myself to be with that experience, that picture, has been meditative in its own way. That's what you are living in – that energy environment. We too can heal, enrich and grow stronger; we too can remain grounded and energised, in the same way as the trees.

❤ Energy is your environment.

And because we can heal, enrich and grow stronger; because it's important for us to remain grounded and energised, we're going to talk a lot about energy and how things *feel*, how *you* feel. We're all part of that exact same life. Allowing ourselves to be led by our feelings means we're working with the energy around us, inside us, and everywhere else in between. Listening to that energy, and how we respond to that energy, is our indicator that we're on track – or not. Energy is naturally free flowing and should naturally make us feel good. If we're not feeling good, we're blocking something. Remember that: *we're* blocking something! If we're not feeling good, that feeling is ours to own and to do something about.

All too often our energy is blocked as a result of the way we deal with the various components of our day, including the situations that arise throughout our day and the people who participate in our day. People generate a lot of negative energy, and many of our day-to-day situations are generated by people; hence, directly and indirectly, people can have a significant effect on our state of being if we are not conscious of protecting ourselves from their energy. It's often our interactions with others that prevent us from achieving natural, free-flowing ease in our lives.

Life wasn't meant to be the continual struggle – the physical, mental, emotional slog – that we've made it. Yes, we can do something about it. We can change the struggle. And we can do that by taking ownership and looking inside.

We're here, you and I, to unblock the blockages, to remove the obstructions in your energy that have formed as a result of the stressors in your life, and to let love and life flow.

When you make changes to your energy, you'll make big changes to the quality of your life. Love is the highest vibration, the highest frequency of energy. So when your energy vibrates at a higher frequency, you will likely be radiating a lot of love, joy, and compassion. Let that knowledge help you to live from and within your heart.

> It followed from the special theory of relativity that mass and
> energy are both but different manifestations of the same thing –
> a somewhat unfamiliar conception for the average mind.[3]
> Albert Einstein

Doodle, Scribble, Create!

Think about situations when you've been able to feel the energy around you. Think of a time when the energy felt positive, and think of a time when the energy felt negative. Sometimes you might have felt cold or hot hands or feet for no apparent reason, or you might have felt tingles, butterflies, shivers, or a feeling of dread. Sometimes people note that their hair stands on end.

Acknowledge the feelings you had during both situations. Doodle, scribble, create what you felt during the positive experience.

Doodle, Scribble, Create!

Feel. Stop and focus on what you're feeling. Don't think or focus on any particular thoughts. See if you can just feel. We'll talk later in the book about how your thoughts affect the way you feel, but for now, just see if you can slow down enough to feel what's going on inside your body. Breathe deeply (you'll learn about that later in the book too) and try and switch off. Focus on something nice. Enjoy it. Tune in to good feelings. Say hi. You've been living in your head your whole life; now is the time to start living in your heart. And you can do this by starting to feel what's going on inside.

Make your feelings good feelings. This is the start of you consciously changing your thought and belief patterns.

Doodle, scribble, create three good feelings that you have right now. Spend some time so that the feelings can sink in. You're already starting to change your momentum.

Chakras and Chakra Blocks

You may have heard of chakras. We're not going to spend a lot of time on chakras in this book, as the chakras are worthy of a focus all their own. However, it's important that you're aware of them because they play such a significant role in your life and the way you are feeling.

I used to see references to chakras in bookshops, spiritual centres, crystal and holistic outlets, and yoga studios. Although I always thought I'd like to know about and understand chakras, I had absolutely no idea what they were, and it took me years to do anything about learning about them. So I mean it when I advise you not to worry if a lot of this is totally new to you. I've made a point of learning about the chakras only during the past few years, and I'm actively focussing on them knowing, now, their impact on my life. I recently trained in chakra dancing so I could help others to understand and experience the power of balanced chakras, and now run chakra dancing classes around my local area.

In your body, there are seven main energy centres. Over a long time in history, these centres have come to be known as chakras. Chakra is a Sanskrit word for 'wheel' or 'centre'. Sanskrit is an ancient language of India. Each chakra encapsulates nerves and organs as well as our state of well-being in certain areas in our body. If any of your chakras is out of tune – or blocked – you won't be operating at your optimal capacity. This is because the parts of your body that correspond with that chakra won't be able to do what they're meant to be doing because the energy can't flow properly through those areas.

Too many of us probably have blockages at most, if not all seven, chakras. And all too many of us don't even know these energy centres exist, never mind the important part they play in our health and well-being. This explains a lot.

Each chakra focuses on a certain aspect of your life. We've come to identify our chakra centres by colours, and this may help you to identify them better and remember where they are in your body. However, while visualising the colours can help with healing and focus on certain chakras, more important is doing what you can to ensure free-flowing energy through each chakra centre. To get a picture of where your chakras are, look online, as there are thousands of images that will help. Otherwise, look for books and even posters in bookshops, especially those that specialise in spiritual and New Age topics. A library could also be a good resource.

Root chakra (Sanskrit name: *Muladhara*): *I am*. This is your first chakra and it's situated at the base of your spine. It's represented by the colour red, and it signifies earth, grounding and your feelings of security, safety, self-preservation, and survival. This chakra always makes me think of what Abraham Maslow identified as our base needs – our basic biological and physiological needs. Your first chakra relates to how secure you feel in all basic areas of your life.

Sacral chakra (*Svadhisthana*): *I feel*. Relate orange to this area between your tummy button and your root chakra area. The sacral chakra signifies the water element and fluidity. It relates to your sense of passion, pleasure, well-being, and abundance, and to how you feel about your relationships and your sexuality. It's the centre for connection, forgiveness, responsibility and emotion, and is a very sensual centre. When your sacral chakra is in balance, it allows you to change and transform, as well as to accept others and new experiences.

Solar plexus (*Manipura*): *I do*. This yellow chakra is about your power. Your will. Your confidence. Your sense of belonging. When your solar plexus chakra is in balance, you feel empowered and assertive; you have a strong degree of self-discipline and a good sense of self-worth and self-esteem. You are listening to *you*, and living true to yourself. Your solar plexus is situated between your ribs and your tummy button and it is the chakra centre that matches up to your ego, keeping it in its place and preventing it from taking over your life. Your lower two chakras correspond with the elements of earth and water; your solar plexus is your fire centre. Think of your inner sunshine.

Heart chakra (*Anahata*): *I love.* Feel harmony within, and accept life. Open your heart. Be giving and feel, be and live love. This chakra is green and is situated in the area of your chest at the middle of your breastbone. Feel the element of air. Breathe deeply and well. Your heart chakra is your centre for compassion, joy, peace and unconditional love, especially for yourself. Many people believe that, if you can live pure love and with a balanced heart chakra, all your other chakras will balance because love represents the highest, most intense form of energy.

Throat chakra (*Vishudha*): *I speak.* We speak, but what do we say? We speak, but do we listen to what we're saying? We speak, but is there wisdom and worth in our words? Honour *you* by living true to your throat chakra and speaking your truth. (And if your heart chakra is in balance, you do so with love and compassion.) The throat chakra is about your ability to communicate and releasing your inner sound. It's about expression and self-expression of feelings and the truth – your truth – and your personal integrity. Situated at the base of the throat, the throat chakra is sky blue and the element is the ether.

Third eye chakra (*Ajna*): *I see.* Your third eye centre is an indigo, purplish colour situated on your forehead between your eyebrows. When balanced, your third eye helps with creativity, imagination, intuition, and wisdom as well as your ability to focus on and see the bigger picture. It also helps with perception, inner vision, insight, self-reflection, and your ability to think clearly and make decisions. Your third eye is your link with the element of light and being open to higher realms of consciousness.

Crown chakra (*Sahasrara*): *I understand.* Your seventh chakra is at the very top of your head – your crown. Your crown chakra is a sacred spot and your centre for divine wisdom. When it's open, unblocked, and in balance, your crown chakra helps you to connect to the higher energy of the universe. It's your energy centre for trust, inner and outer beauty, awareness, understanding, and feeling happy and positive. Up there, at your crown, this chakra is usually considered violet, or white, and sometimes pink. You'll often see it represented by the lotus flower.

💗 Your seven energy centres affect your well-being.

When I first learned about the chakras, I was stunned that we're not taught about them at school. As I've learned more and more about our bodies, our universe, and how everything works, I've been bemused, dismayed, and completely baffled, time and time again, at what we're *not* taught and what we *don't* know about our bodies, our energy, and how everything works. Why wouldn't we want to know that, if we're experiencing lower back pain, it could be related to an imbalance or blockage at our root chakra!

I couldn't understand why I'd had to find out all about the chakras of my own accord, as part of my own adventure, somewhere during my forties! We're taught a limited amount about our organs and body 'systems'; in fact, we receive a very basic amount of information about our human bodies during our early years of schooling, but we're given nothing whatsoever about the existence of our energy centres, despite how important they are.

That is because we can't see them. In this life, in our Western society, if you can't see something, it doesn't exist. And this adds way too much fuel to my discussion later on about why we're not encouraged to *feel*. Yet, if you can turn that belief around, understand that there's so much more in our world than simply what we can see or perceive, you'll feel and inherently be able to recognise whether your energy body is in balance or not.

There's a *lot* to be said about functioning and malfunctioning chakras – or clear, flowing, clean energy chakras versus centres of blocked, stagnant energy. Even just starting to be aware of your chakras and having a basic understanding of their purpose can work wonders for your sense of wellness. For example, I bought myself a heart-chakra mouse pad. I'm at my computer a lot of the time, so having a subtle reminder next to me reminds me to relax; open my heart; feel patience, love and joy; and allow flow. I also picked up a few individual chakra-related yoga stretches, which I often do at home, and I focus on when things feel *right* so I can identify what *right* feels like and where in my body it feels right. This helps me to recognise which chakra centres are in balance.

Reiki can help to balance your chakras; what you eat and drink can help to balance your chakras; reviewing your relationships, your beliefs, and what you say, do, and think can help to balance your chakras.

This information only scratches the surface. Your chakras are a part of you that deserves acknowledgement and attention. They have a significant effect on your health and well-being.

♥ Balanced chakras mean a balanced, healthy *you*.

Doodle, Scribble, Create!

Choose something from the information I've presented about the universe, energy, and chakras that you'd like to know more about and do a little research. It might be an idea that resonates with you or an idea that goes against everything you believe. It might be something that tickled your curiosity, or it might be something you've simply never heard of that you realise you'd like to know more about. It might be something that you've heard of but that you've always denied, ignored, or condemned because it's not 'normal thinking'. Challenge yourself. Go and find out more about it.

Doodle, scribble, create what you find out.

Is it confronting? Is it informing? Is it eye opening? Is some of it making sense? Does it explain anything? How are you reacting? Does it make you feel comfortable or uncomfortable? Does it feel right? Are you scoffing and ridiculing? Does it make you say 'wow'?

Challenge your thinking through colour and creation. You might take days over this exercise; you might take a whole lifetime as it starts to open you up to a bigger picture and to a wealth of evolving information and learning through which you can really change your quality of life. As you research, pay attention to what's going on inside. Listen. Feel. Don't just stop at one topic; open your mind and go further and further. This is about continuing your adventure with information and support that feels right for you. If it doesn't feel right, keep clicking around until you find what feels right for you, and you get a sense of what all this is about and how you can use it to your benefit.

Doodle, Scribble, Create!

As you build research and continual investigation and growing knowledge into your life, doodle, scribble, create the main three factors that you know you were meant to take from the last exercise. Feel inside for the answers. How are you going to use them to help to start changing your life? How can you – and will you – consciously apply to your day what you're finding out?

*W*e All Have Free Will

SO, YOU'VE GOT USED TO THE fact that you're part of the universe and of universal energy – part of the larger source that is all of us. And you're dabbling with the fact that we're all vibrational and that that's what links us and connects us to everything else that's vibrational. Energy is vibrational; hence, everything is connected. Being aware of that is one step towards feeling better. You're not alone, and life isn't happening to you. You're part of something bigger, and that bigger energy gives you power – if you want to use it to your benefit. That power is your light. It's you, it's your intuition, your authentic self. It's the balance of your solar plexus chakra, and that power gives you a healthy self-esteem, purpose, and the confidence and will to assert your self and to embrace responsibility for what happens in your life. You'll gradually listen to – and heed – your inner self, and that is what will help you feel better.

The point of this next section is to remind you that you were born with the free will to make choices. In many cases, because we are products of our environments, it may seem that we don't. Yet without free will, what *do* we have? With free will we have power; with free will we own our own adventures! With free will we can take responsibility and be assertive and accountable.

With free will we can be strong, we can make our own choices, and we can *shine our lights*.

Choosing to disregard or ignore your free will means life will happen to you. Don't make excuses. Reclaim your free will and make this *your* life.

In all the learning, reading, and experiencing of life I've done over the years, it's only fairly recently that I've really digested just how significant free will is in terms of all of us being and living true to ourselves. Of course, we do believe that throughout our days we're making our own choices, but often we're doing so just as long as it suits us. We can be a bit selective. How often do you hear yourself and others state, 'I had no choice'. You have a choice in everything you do. And don't say, 'Ah, but ...' You have the choice to be in the job you are doing. Don't forget that you chose to take that job, and at the moment, you are choosing to stay in it. You have the choice to speak up for yourself. You have the choice to question everything you were brought up to be. You have the choice not to be a victim of your upbringing but to use your knowledge and experiences to serve you and others. You have the choice to believe you are just as good and just as worthy as others (which you *are*). You have the choice to be pursuing more money, or going out more, or staying in more, or changing your circle of friends. You have the choice to decide what to believe, and you have the choice over what you think and say.

You have the choice to believe you can change your environment, yourself, your world.

♥ What to believe is your choice. Have you reviewed your beliefs lately?

'I felt I should' or 'I thought I'd better' (or 'I'd better not') are resounding statements of reason we use for sticking with our lot and then complaining about it. Yet what life might you have if you remembered, acknowledged, and took responsibility for the fact that you *do* have a choice. Every time you say you had no choice, you're making the choice to let your life happen to you instead of taking the lead and creating what you want in and from your life.

Responsibility for your life is your own choice. Remembering you have the power to make your own choices makes your solar plexus chakra happy.

The Choice is Yours

When we do make conscious choices, many of us make them based on how we've been brought up and what's expected of us, just as our parents and their parents have done before us. Few of us make choices based on what actually feels right for us, and so we become products of our upbringing and our societies. My dad wanted to become a professional golfer, but my gran didn't let him pursue that career. A friend of mine wanted to learn a trade, but to keep up with the social stature his family perceived to be more important than his pursuit of his personal desires and dreams, he was pressured into going to university to study law. Not surprisingly, he dropped out of school, got sick, and eventually went on to do something much more suited to his own personal adventure, truth, feelings, and desires.

Because generations of us have allowed ourselves to be chewed up and controlled by what's apparently expected of us – which doesn't appear to have served us up much to smile about – we have given up our ability to use our true free will; so much so that often we don't even know what it is we believe in, or what choices we would make if we weren't allowing others to make or dictate them for us. With all the conforming, we have lost our authenticity; we have lost track of who we really are, who we wanted to be, and who we can be, because we were conditioned to be regulated, and we became suffocated by 'what we *should* be doing'.

Gran's spirit is now calling for us all to let out our inner golfer!

We've grown so accustomed to doing what's going to keep the waters calm that we fear doing things any other way. So we continue in this cycle of events, conforming and feeling chained, sinking deeper and deeper, attracting more and more of the same, unable to see what really *is*, and wondering if and when we'll ever feel free to be ourselves. It becomes easier and more natural to blame the world for our lot than it does to stand up for ourselves, take responsibility, and speak and live our truth. Our ego selves are so busy keeping up with each other on the social, material, and consumer hierarchy of greed and 'need', that our true selves are a faint whisper with little to no chance of being heard against such nurturing of ego mania. So long as we're putting so much effort into trying to be the something or somebody we think we need to be, or into worrying that we're *not* what we think we need to be, our little lights inside, as they try to send us messages, struggle to be seen, felt, or even acknowledged.

Cue my friend, Heather, who often sings 'This little light of mine, I'm going to let it shine …'

And because we're so quick to judge and put others down, we know that others are doing the same to us, so we're too scared to do anything outside the norm. We do little to challenge what those around us are saying, or what others think we should be doing, wearing, or saying. Hence, we do nothing, and hence we become resentful, frustrated, fed up, and stuck in a rut. And hence we have mid- or late-life crises and regrets, and we wonder about what would have happened if only we'd gone with what felt right. We've all heard of dying people having regrets. Don't let that be you.

♥ Let your inner golfer out!

Free will is about living the authentic you. Free will is about making choices that serve *you* and not your ego. Your ego persuades you, usually without too much effort, to make choices that are based on fear. Your ego prompts you towards doubting yourself and towards meeting the judgements and expectations of others. Choose to listen inside and follow what you're drawn to and what feels right instead of looking outside for reasons and excuses not to.

Choose to follow your heart instead of your ego.

Then hang on to your hat and fly, earth angel. You're not alone. You *can* do it. There's nothing to stop you but yourself. There are no valid excuses. Go at your own pace, and start feeling freer than you ever have.

Decisions, Decisions ...

Before we focus on a specific exercise, let's think through something.

Think about everything in your life right now. Somewhere, you will have a decision to make about something. It doesn't matter if it's major or minor. It might be about your career or your house; it might be about your shopping list or whether to buy those trousers. It might be whether to take the dog out now or later, if you should hang the washing out, or what day to do something you need to do. It doesn't matter what it is.

What's your *immediate* feeling about that decision? Before you even think about it, what *feels* right? This way or that way? Now or later? Yes or no? What answer came to you before you even finished asking yourself the question?

Now *think* about it.

Does the feeling about the decision change? Why is that? What factors are you taking into account?

Here's an example of what I allow my ego to do to me: I've got a stretch of a few hours ahead, and I know, deep down, that for *me*, I need to go out for a walk and breathe in some nature and fresh air.

Ego: But you've only got three hours. You should sit down and work on that book!

Me: But I don't feel like writing. The dog and I need out.

Ego: But, if you take the dog out you'll lose an hour or two, and then you won't get as much writing done.

Me: Okay. I'll sit down and start writing.

Ego: But, if you don't feel like it, you know you won't get anything done. You'd be able to think better after some fresh air.

Me: Okay. I'll go and get some fresh air.

Ego: But you'll stay out too long and won't get any writing done.

Me: Shut *up!*

It's a wonder you've got this book in your hands the way my heart and head sometimes go at each other. In that situation I absolutely should go out. It's what my immediate feeling is, and it's what my deep knowing is. I *need* to go out. That's why it can get so frustrating 'being in your own head'. I *know* at times like this that, if I've not already been out and got my dose of nature and fresh air, I'm going to achieve nothing staying in trying to force things to happen. (Later, in Part Two, I share my thoughts about force as a form of resistance. Force doesn't serve you.) Without that break, I'm going to be distracted, frustrated, and drained. I know that I need fresh air and exercise to be able to write in the first place, so I also know that there's absolutely no point even attempting to spend the few hours writing. And if I sit down and force it, I'll do just as much in eight hours as I'd do in four (if not two) and I won't like what I've written so I'll be back to square one.

During the course of writing this book, however, I've got so much better. And so can you. We're changing habits of a lifetime, and until we pay attention to what we're putting ourselves through by listening only to our heads and not our feelings – our hearts – we don't change anything. Now I go out and often also try to do a bit of yoga or a meditation before I get started. I've realised and accepted that I work best after I've cleared my head and nurtured my body. I've learned that it's fine not to start work until late morning or even lunchtime.

Be aware of faffing (dithering) about making decisions that your heart already knows the answer to. I used to procrastinate so much over small decisions that I'd achieve nothing at all during those few hours other than feeling tired, drained, and frustrated. In the walk versus work situation, even though I'd looked inside for – and knew – my answer, I *still* fought that battle with my ego instead of just going and doing what I knew I needed to do.

❤ Nike's got a point – Just *do* it!

So there's what I'm getting at: the subtleties within your day. You're making choices and decisions all day long, but you probably don't notice half of them. When you consciously pay attention to what you're doing and what you're thinking, you realise that there's a choice in every part of your day. You're choosing to eat that cake. You're choosing to get up so late that you have to rush or you miss the bus. You're choosing to think the thoughts you're thinking. You're choosing to allow the bad feelings you're experiencing.

Deep down inside, does it feel more right to do that or do this? To go that way or this way? Deep down inside, what messages are you receiving about your adventure, about your day, about any given situation? Deep down inside, you know these trousers don't suit you, or that they're the wrong colour, or that you probably won't wear them. 'But they're the right price.' 'But you won't wear them. You don't like them that much.' 'But they're the right price …'

And so it goes on.

You beat down the overgrowth to make your way unwillingly forward in the same direction yet again, when you could stroll along a country path in the sunshine, open and content and with belief in yourself, confidence and faith in your decisions, and trust that the universe will bring you what you need if and when you need it.

For You or For Them …

The thing is, you probably know loudly and clearly what the *right* decision for you is in many situations; yet you will procrastinate over the decision based on what other people might think or expect, or whether your decision will hurt them or make them feel upset or insulted or let down. Or you'll be worrying about what will happen if it goes wrong. What if it's the 'wrong' decision? What if you don't enjoy it? What if it hurts? You get the idea.

Is everything on your food shopping list for everyone else in your family? Is there anything on it that you actually enjoy eating? Are you staying in the same job because it's safe or because others say you're lucky and should be happy with what you've got? Are you going on holiday to a certain place to keep the peace? Are you eating a piece of cake because someone made it especially for you but you don't actually want it or like it, and the provider might be offended?

Some of these questions don't feel as if they represent conscious decisions, but every single one of them is a scenario in which you can make your own choice. You could eat your bowl of pasta with chopsticks if you wanted to. You could dress in whatever colours you want. You could say 'no thank you'. You could stop for a minute and think about what it is you want to choose in your life to make you smile more.

Oh, but then you'd be selfish. Or people would talk about you. Or you'd feel silly, or guilty. So you conform. You live within the mould. You do what is 'right' and 'expected'; you don't like to 'rock the boat' or say 'no'. You choose to live in whatever way attracts as little embarrassment, judgement, criticism, and confrontation as you can.

And it doesn't make you happy. It doesn't make you feel good.

The purpose of this section is to help you become aware of every decision you make on a daily basis, consciously or subconsciously, big or small.

If it *feels* like the right decision for you, then make the decision and get on with it. Procrastination and over analysis by your ego are stifling and oppressive. I know. I used to be a master of the two. How freeing it is to just make a decision or a choice and keep your life moving!

We allow doubt and the judgements of other people to be the main reason we don't use our free will to serve us. We think 'ah but' or 'what if' and then we do nothing. But what if you made a decision to do something different, or to change something, and it goes right? What if it's exactly the *right* decision? What if others look at you and wish they had your courage, your faith and belief in themselves, your optimism, your positive outlook and your perspective? What if, what if, what if …

This isn't about making decisions only for yourself without considering anybody else. It's about weighing up why you make the decisions you make and about asserting your own power over the choices you have, and then accepting the decisions and choices that you've made and learning from them where necessary.

♥ Listen to your heart. It knows every answer.

Doodle, Scribble, Create!

Doodle, scribble, create your free will world. Consider what it's been up till now and then create loudly and clearly what it's going to be from now on.

And then specifically create the answer, the decision. Make the choice about something that's going on in your life right now — and stick with that decision.

Benefiting from the Law of Attraction

THERE ARE A NUMBER OF UNIVERSAL laws all working within the energy field and affecting your life. The law of free will is one. Another is the law of attraction. Another is the law of vibration.

The law of attraction states that you attract more of the same type of vibrational energy that you give out. What you focus on attracts energy. You might have heard phrases like 'like attracts like' or 'where your attention goes, your energy flows'.

What words, emotions, and attitudes do you habitually convey? This law helps to explain why some people 'have it good' and some people don't. If you're a right old misery guts about your life, and do nothing but whinge and complain about your lot, bringing everyone else down around you, then you're doing yourself a disfavour – no, not just a disfavour; you're doing yourself a mighty disservice, and doing everything right to make sure you attract more to make yourself miserable.

Yet, if you look on the bright side and accept that every experience – whatever the experience – is an important part of your growth and your adventure, and that it's only your reaction, the way you deal with life, that makes the difference, you can identify what needs to change and you could attract far more positive experiences to your life.

Nobody and nothing is out to get you.

♥ It's not the situation, but your reaction that matters.

The law of attraction is about getting back what you put out. It's said to be a three-step process: ask, believe, receive.

Universal energy brings you what you're asking for. That doesn't mean you literally have to 'ask', although that does no harm at all. It just means that you will receive more of whatever you are *being*, whatever you are *living*, whatever attitudes, moods, and emotions you are *exuding*. Your emotions, your words, the feelings you're creating from your thoughts – all of these combine to ensure that you get what you're focussing on. Which is why, if you are continually jaded, feeling as if you have no choice, listening to your ego telling you how hard everything is and how bad you are at it all, you will continue along that path.

Whereas, you will live a happier life and attract more of the same if you put out friendly thoughts; smile and see the positive side of things; enjoy the small things in life; appreciate the beauty in nature and the world around you; believe that life is good and that experiences are learning opportunities; have a good attitude; are kind, compassionate, caring; don't judge or criticise, but simply accept; and appreciate everything that comes your way for what it is and what you learn from it.

Part of the attraction process is about believing, having faith, and *trusting* that what you would like you can have. And believing and having faith means quashing the doubt you have in your own ability before it gets a hold on you. You must erase the cynicism and lack of belief you're used to feeling about a lot of things. You are fed these negative feelings both by yourself and by those around you. You need to combine belief and faith with *feelings* of belief and faith. Your feelings and emotions are energetically stronger than your mind. Your true feelings are good; they serve you, and they come from deep within *you*. Your bad feelings come from the mind, from your thoughts. Run with thoughts that feel good, full of hope, truth, and honesty, thoughts that lead to feelings of excitement and butterflies. Run with those that feel *right*. And if there's not enough of those, find a way to make more because you *can* change your thoughts. You'll learn how to do that as you work through this book and practise new behaviours.

Feel from your heart, live through your heart, live with love and you'll attract nicer, more loving, heart-felt experiences and better, more enjoyable, results from your endeavours.

> 💜 Your feelings and emotions are energetically stronger than your mind.

This may come across as a little repetitive, but it's an important message and one that can be difficult to truly grasp until you experience the results. *Feelings* are key. If you decide you want to have more to smile about, and deep inside you don't actually believe that will happen, and you do not do anything about making it happen, then it won't happen. However, if you can radiate that you *already have* plenty to smile about, feel and believe that more will come about for you to smile about, and then leave it alone and don't focus on the fact that you haven't *got* anything to smile about, then gradually, with your conscious daily practice of displaying more positive actions and reactions, you'll have more things to smile about.

This is definitely experiential learning, so start doing it today. Pay attention to what you're focusing on. You'll find at first that you can *speak* your good intentions, but if you're honest with yourself you won't be genuinely *believing* in them inside. Until you genuinely believe that you're going to have a good day, that you're going to have a smooth meeting with your boss, that you're going to get through your day hitch free, and properly *feel* it, your words and thoughts alone won't bring you the smiles. It takes time, patience, focus, and attention as well as the powers of intention and visualisation, which I talk about in Part Two.

The law of attraction basically means, for example, that if you're radiating cynicism, negativity, and a lack of something, then you will continue to attract things that confirm cynicism, negativity, and lack. Whereas, if you radiate, say, a carefree smiling persona, you will attract less stress and more joy – and more joyful people – to your life. You will gradually become more easy-going, gracious, and accepting as you shrug off the weighty thoughts you used to tend and feed.

I also talk about believing and receiving in Part Two.

> ♥ You attract what you focus on – believe it will be, and it will be.

What You Focus On ...

Here's a two-fold example of how the law of attraction works. This example shows the positive and the negative results of the law of attraction at work.

I decided I wanted to work part time. I felt that life was too short to be spending so much time at work. I had no idea how or where I was going to find part-time work. I began to focus on one particular opportunity that I'd decided was perfect, that I'd decided I *needed* in order to manage my own hours. But that job wasn't opening up for me, and I wasn't doing anything at all to find other part-time work. I was just becoming more and more frustrated that the supposed perfect opportunity wasn't happening.

And the more frustrated I became that the perfect opportunity wasn't being offered to me, the more I began questioning – what was this law of attraction! I was believing I would be offered the perfect opportunity. That's what I was supposed to do! I became more and more frustrated and angry about everything that went with the five-day, over-forty-one-hours-a-week job I was doing at the time. I became a very miserable person, both to myself and to others.

This went on for about six weeks when, finally, I took back ownership of my emotions, my choices, and my life. I resigned from my current job. I'd had such continual negative feelings about that particular job that it was draining my spirit, and I knew I had to make changes. Nothing had happened in relation to the 'perfect opportunity', and I was allowing my whole life to be affected by the job I was doing.

Once I had released all of my resistance by accepting that the perfect opportunity wasn't coming my way, and once I had let go of (by resigning) the second thing that was bringing me down, my mind, body, and spirit opened up to fully and wholly allow other things in. When you're living so stressed, so angry, so full of doubt, so overwhelmed, and so focused on the *lack* of something you want and need, you put up a very strong barrier – resistance. And that barrier shuts out everything you genuinely desire and prevents what you want from coming your way.

I was never going to have that perfect opportunity offered to me. Look at the way my attitude was towards it! At the time I was living in my own little angry world and actually thought I was focusing on the perfect opportunity correctly. But, indeed, I was focusing on in it in all the wrong ways. I was stuck on the fact that it *wasn't* there. I was angry and frustrated and confused about the fact that it wasn't happening. These emotions positively ensure that what you desire won't be forthcoming. And I was stuck on the fact, every day, that it was what I *wanted* but that it wasn't here. No part of me was feeling positive. No part of me was extending loving feelings about new opportunities; in fact, a new opportunity was only a means of escaping from my full-time job; hence, it was never going to be right for me anyway.

In the meantime, I had developed a very strong belief that I would work part time; I wasn't in any doubt about that. I had verbalised that on numerous occasions, believed it would happen, and I had done *nothing* to get myself stuck on how or when it would happen, or the fact that it wasn't happening just then. I just quietly believed it would happen and left it alone.

So, most of the story so far has been about the negative effects of the law of attraction at work. Here's the positive effect: several days after receiving my letter of resignation, my boss offered me the opportunity to stay and reduce my time to four days with no Saturday overtime. There were two additional major aspects of the offer my boss made me, and I felt incredibly thankful and so appreciative. That had been my intention – to work part time! I had pictured it, I had believed it would happen, I'd had faith in my decision, and I hadn't got stuck on focussing on how it was going to happen or the fact that it *wasn't* happening. I hadn't been specific about where or how it would happen, and I certainly hadn't expected it to come from precisely the place I was resigning from.

You really can create your life. It works the same way for you.

♥ Pull down your walls of resistance. Open your heart and create your world.

Doodle, Scribble, Create!

Consider the section you've just read on the law of attraction. On their own, the words can't teach you anything. The best way for you to identify with attraction-based living is to think about the times you've generated good outcomes in your life. And think of some times when you've generated less enjoyable outcomes.

Doodle, scribble, create what the law of attraction means to you, having read the brief account I presented here. Include any other research or reading you've done on the subject. What has it meant to your life to date? There will have been positive and negative outcomes over the years.

More importantly, what do you feel it means in your life now? As you create with your colours, let your pencils flow. Choose colours that describe how you're going to become more conscious of the law of attraction and use it in ways that serve you.

Being Grateful

One of the main ways you can help the law of attraction work in your favour is by being grateful. Appreciating everything you have in your life is a powerful way to generate more things to be thankful for.

Thank *you* for being here with me reading this book. Thank you, universe, for bringing me to another day with my home comforts, my health, and people who love me. Thank you for 'my trees' – the two trees that inspire me and ground me as soon as I open my curtains in the morning.

Thank you, Mr A, for offering me part-time work. Thank you, Stan K, for offering me full-time work in Australia and giving me a go on the other side of the world. Thank you, Liz V, for believing in me and giving me so many exciting opportunities. Thank you, Mum and Dad, for teaching me honesty and choices. Thank you, David, for encouraging me to be myself. Thank you, universe, for giving me what I needed to get this book out to the world and for telling me I needed to do it in the first place. Thank you, Balboa Press, for helping me to publish it. Thank you, special Meadow Linn, for endorsing it.

Thank you, world, for every single experience I've ever had that has brought me to where I am now, able to sit here offering guidance, inspiration, and the chance of empowerment to others who might be able to use the encouragement to their benefit. Thank you, *me*, for helping me to listen, and for helping me to step over, past, and through the fear of taking myself public. Thank you, thank you, thank you – all day, every day – thank you!

♥ Thank you.

In 2007, I learned from Rhonda Byrne's movie, *The Secret*[4], about the law of attraction and the importance of being grateful, of appreciating, and of giving thanks for everything that comes our way – and, indeed, everything we'd like to come our way. (It was the original version of this movie that introduced me to Esther Hicks who was channelling the non-physical entity Abraham throughout her presentation.)

This section is easy. Being grateful is easy. The difficult bit at first is that you need to *feel* thankful for things in your life, and you need to make a conscious effort – just like everything we're talking about here – to build that appreciation into your day. And that means becoming conscious of things in your day to be thankful for. And believe me, there are plenty of them. You'll become aware of plenty things to value once you pay attention.

As you identify things, experiences, and people that you are grateful for, really *feel* that gratefulness. It could be that you're grateful to be breathing without having to think about it. It could be that you appreciate a kindness someone showed to you today. It could be giving thanks that your car started, that the birds are chirping, and that the breeze is blowing through the trees. It could be giving thanks for finding your keys, for your day going smoothly, for how you dealt with a situation. It can be everything and anything. Today I put out thanks for the time I spent catching up with my friend, for the perfection of the colourful new buds on a bush, and for finding the dog's frisbee in the long grass. We *need* that frisbee!

Do that now. Recognise things in and around your life that you appreciate, and *feel* your deeply rooted thanks for these things.

Doodle, Scribble, Create!

Doodle, scribble, create a big thank you for
at least five things in your life.

As you're doodling really start to feel what these
things – or people, or experiences – mean to you.

Building Appreciation into Your Day

Building appreciation into your day needs to be a conscious and heart-felt exercise. Only you know the best way for you to start doing this. When I first started doing it, I did it when I went to bed at night, and I thought back to everything and everybody that had happened in my day as well as things that were stable and positive in my life. I found I had to try to pay conscious attention during the day and take note of things that made me smile or made me happy: someone saying hello, seeing someone serve a kindness on another, hearing the sounds of the birds, watching a bumble bee busy at work, watching trains running smoothly and on time, someone buying me a coffee. I used to try to write down five things, but very quickly I would be writing down twenty or thirty aspects of my day and my life that were positive and for which I felt very blessed.

We have a plaque on the wall at home that says 'Every day may not be good, but there is something good in every day.' Every day serves you up a lot more than 'something' good. Every day serves you up more than you can imagine. Really pay attention to what's good and decent in your life, and stop focussing on what's not serving you. You'll find joys you didn't realise were there.

Nowadays I give heart-felt thanks and appreciation before I even get out of bed. I have four safe walls around me. I have woken up and the sun has risen. I am cosy, comfy, and warm, and I feel very, very blessed. It's a great way to start the day, and it has become very natural for me. I do it again once I've left the house and I'm on my way to wherever I'm going. These two early-day bursts help me set up my day.

And because I've now formed the habit and don't have to think about it, I do it throughout the day, every single time something works for me, somebody helps me, and something goes well. It's become a regular activity, and it happens easily because I *am* thankful for so much of what I have and what comes my way.

♥ Thank you.

You can do this too. You'll find that gradually you too will offer up 'thank you' regularly and generously throughout your day. Occasionally, during a short walk I used to take to work, I'd spend the entire twenty minutes thanking the universe for the beauty and ease in my life. I found it difficult at first to do that consciously, but once you can shut off your head – your ego – you can take in what's around you. If you can stick with that for about half a minute, you can gain a momentum that can keep you going for quite a significant amount of time. I'd be thankful for the scenic walk I had to work, the fact that I *could* walk to work, the fact that I had a job to walk to in the first place, a regular monthly income. I'd be thankful for the experiences that were going to be forthcoming in my day ahead, the fact that I was breathing and alive and surrounded by so much fresh, clean air and natural, seasonal life. I'd thank my neighbour for his garden and the sweet smells coming from his flora. I literally did stop and smell the roses – and the lavender, the hyacinths, the sweet peas. I still do when I pass by. Thank you, Johnnie!

Stop. Stop and look around you. Take in the beauty and the wonder. Take in the view, the sights. Breathe the fresh air deep down into your inner depths. Look at the robin, *listen* to the robin, *watch* the robin, imagine *being* the robin. Take in the trees, properly look at the petals on the daffodil, delight in the blossom of spring. Stop and watch the squirrel, the ant, the butterfly, the bumble bee, *look* at the colours, inhale the sweet smells of the season, inhale your surroundings.

Breathe in the atmosphere. Rejoice to the sky, to the sun, to the buildings that house you. Look at the light and notice how it changes from day to day, season to season, hour to hour. Breathe in so deeply that your tummy fills up and sticks out, and notice how good that actually feels.

Give thanks for the fact that you are breathing your way through life without even trying. Give thanks for what your body does for you without you having to pay very much attention at all. In fact, think of some of the potentially negative things you *do* do to your body, and give big thanks for what your body is doing, without your assistance, to counteract them.

Give thanks for the fact that you have a place to live, you have heat, food, and light. What about the transport you have: car, bus, bicycle, legs, wheelchair. They're all working for you; they are there to take you where you want to go.

Be thankful. Make it your middle name. Be grateful every single day for every good thing that comes your way, big or small, major or minor. Once you've started this you'll get better and better at it and you'll really notice how often you're saying it – and *feeling* it – in your day. You've got nothing to lose and everything to gain. By being consciously and consistently grateful, you're also focussing on the positive, and that alone takes the focus off the negative, which gradually falls away and becomes less noticeable.

Appreciation turns your life around.

♥ Thank you.

Doodle, Scribble, Create!

Doodle, scribble, create as many things as you can think of that you are thankful for. Show your true and genuine appreciation for all the greatness you do actually have in your life.

Thank Someone in Writing

I've just remembered writing to the Berol pen company when I was in my teens to thank them for a brilliant pen I had bought. I loved the colour of it and the way it wrote. The company sent me another of the pens and a nice letter. So way back then, before I had any idea that being thankful for my lot could actually benefit me in return, I had frequent and regular periods of living with thanks and gratitude, living the law of attraction, living love instead of fear.

Actually, although I say I wasn't aware that being thankful could benefit me in return, I had realised from an experience I'd had when I was nine that taking things people gave me for granted made me feel sick, guilty, and horrible inside. My mum had hand made me a big selection of clothes for my Sindy doll for Christmas, and I swapped some of them with a girl around whom I felt a little intimidated. Straight after I'd done it, I wished I could undo it but the girl had gone. From feeling those negative feelings for the first time in my life (that I can remember), I very quickly became genuinely appreciative of gifts that people gave me. I'd loved those clothes, and I'd loved that Mum had made them for me. I didn't want these consequent feelings that came with taking something for granted.

We all have periods of living with thanks and gratitude, living love instead of fear. Even though we're not always doing it consciously, we *do* do things that attract positive creations. Imagine what we can do if we pay attention!

So do that today. Give thanks to someone in writing. In fact, do it right now. Cards are nice, hand-written is nice, but e-mail or text is better than nothing if that will make sure you do it. Thank someone in writing for what they bring to your life. It might be a great pen. It might be that the person makes you laugh. It might be that you can simply trust this person. It can be enough that you love someone and want to thank them for having you in their life, or to thank them for being in yours.

❤ Thank you.

I thanked my publishing consultant recently, not just for calling me to clarify something he'd sent me in an e-mail that he wasn't happy with, but for listening to my questions and comments fully before responding. This is a hugely respectful trait, as there's often not a lot of listening going on out there. Pay attention to that. You'll see a lot of interrupting, a lack of true listening to and acknowledgement of what someone is saying. You'll see a lot of people pre-empting what someone is going to say, interrupting, and then turning the conversation onto themselves! There are a lot of throat chakras out of whack out there.

Really listen to what somebody is telling you today, and give the person a reason to be thankful to you for really listening and properly hearing what they are saying. Silence is golden when it comes to communication. Listening is part of communicating. And don't forget to offer up some appreciation for the fact that the person had a reason to tell *you* what they wanted to tell you in the first place.

Have you written your thank you yet? I just texted my friend. I said, 'Thank you very much for your friendship, for accepting me as I am, for making me laugh, for sharing some of you with me and for having no assumptions or expectations of me. I hope you're having a lovely weekend. Hearts and flowers. xxx'

Now go on, do it. You've no excuses. Get out of your comfort zone and show someone you care. Bring more thanks into your world. Someone will be glad you did. Starting to *do* the right things will help the genuine *feelings* to develop.

❤ Thank you.

Taking Advantage of Momentum

Let's dig a bit deeper on the appreciation angle. You can give thanks, thanks, and more thanks, but knowing a bit more of the context will help you understand why some things are easy and others are difficult.

Overnight, while you're sleeping, your body loses its momentum; your head clears, and your body rests. That's right. As you sleep, your head clears.

Yet what do we do with that? Almost automatically, as soon as we wake up, we go straight back to thinking about what was going on yesterday, or we delve into worrying about things that either won't happen or that we can't do anything about.

So, as well as offering up thanks and appreciation in and for your day, the better you become at not *immediately* going back to what was going on yesterday, or taking a nose dive into everything that's potentially and perceivably bad, the better ready you'll be to set yourself up for today and the better able you'll be to cope with what's on today. Of course whatever's going on from yesterday will still be there, but you can choose how you react to it, how you deal with it, how you proceed through the next stage of it. You'll also be able to choose when you'll be ready to think about it again. Remember? Free will? Every single minute of every single day you have choices.

Rather than allowing yesterday to take hold of you as soon as you wake up, you can take ownership of your thoughts – of yesterday and today – and consider consciously how you will allow the next stage to unfold. Conscious thought and intention will begin to play a bigger role in your life. You don't have to think about everything that's a struggle in your life. In fact, once you start thinking and feeling differently, and using your discipline and empowerment, you'll find things to be less of a struggle than they seem to be now.

However, if you're anything like I used to be, you'll be straight back into whatever's been going on in your life and whatever it was you were worrying about yesterday before you've even had a chance to properly open your eyes. Your ego will have bashed its way through your subconscious, reminded you what day it is and where you're at, and be waving its big negative ego flag as you drag yourself from your amazing slumber before you – *you* – have even had a look in.

I'm not joking about that. I remember years ago wakening up one particular morning. I must have had a really good sleep because I'd had time to properly lose momentum from the day before and wake up feeling very refreshed. Yet I wasn't used to still having the clear, empty-head momentum literally moments after I'd woken up – the clear, empty-head momentum that makes you feel alive, amazing and inspired to realise that, 'Wow! It really *is* a brand new day!' I was almost confused as I became aware of, and processed the fact, that there was actually nothing in my head.

So what did I do with that moment of bliss? Did I take time to just be with that feeling, to enjoy being in the present moment, to appreciate my surroundings and everything I had in my life and set creative intentions for a wonderful day?

Ha ha! Very good. No! The conscious thought didn't even get a look in. Get this: I *made* myself think back to whatever it was that was going on yesterday. I actually thought, 'What was it that was going on again? What was it I was worrying about? What am I supposed to be thinking about?' And, of course, that opened the floodgates for all the negativity to gush through and take hold of me all over again.

It astounds me when I think about it. Yet that's how we are programmed! I've learned from various articles and journals and speakers that ninety per cent of our thoughts each day are thoughts we thought the day before. *Ninety* per cent! And I don't need science to tell me whether that's right or not. As soon as I heard it and applied it to myself, I had no reason whatsoever to doubt it. So, if thoughts lead to actions and feelings, and repetition of the same thoughts, actions, and feelings every day forms our habits … Well, the picture becomes clear. There's the answer to our 'bad' habits and why we're attracting what we're attracting to our lives.

So, anyway, I realised there was something not very smart about what I was doing to myself each and every day when I first woke up, without even consciously thinking about it or setting out to make it that way.

I gradually changed my thinking patterns so they would serve me, love me, and help guide me instead of fight me, put fear in me, and put me off even getting out of bed in the first place.

When I say I gradually changed, though, I mean I *gradually* changed. I didn't just have this amazing epiphany and then change my ways at the snap of a finger. No way. In fact, by gradually, I mean *eventually*. Eventually I became more consistent and more conscious about my thoughts and how they were making me feel.

And by eventually, I mean *years* later.

Allow Yourself to Receive

There's one more thing that's linked with the law of attraction and being thankful, and that's allowing yourself to receive what's coming your way. You must trust that your desires will come and open up to allow them in. Yet lo and behold, as the humans that we are, we're better at expecting and welcoming the fear, the guilt, the worry, the embarrassment, the doubt, the anger, the blow to our confidence than we are at believing we'll receive – and welcoming – a beneficial return of our attitude of appreciation and thanks.

So, to make all of this easier, as you give thanks, be open to receiving 'thanks' back. Stop expecting the worst, and if you can't expect good or better, expect nothing – at least that way you'll be neutral. Because the law of attraction works so well, you'll be better off neutral than negative!

In Part Two, I'll share how you *can* become more open and more accepting of the good things that you're attracting – or are trying to attract – to your life.

> ♥ Use momentum to serve you, and allow
> yourself to receive your dreams.

Doodle, Scribble, Create!

1.   Doodle, scribble, create the name of the person you're writing to thank, and the reason you're writing to thank them. Say thank you loudly, clearly, and in colour; really feel what the person means to you.

2.   Doodle, scribble, create the feeling you get when you open up and 'allow' something different into your life. Now that you're being more thankful, and giving out positive vibes of appreciation, create in colour what it feels like to be experimenting with true, heart-felt thanks, appreciation, and gratitude.

L ove and Fear

YOU MAY HAVE NOTICED SUBTLE REFERENCES to the words *love* and *fear* up till now. From here on, I'm going to refer a lot to these polar-opposite emotions. Much of what I've read and listened to over the past ten to fifteen years suggests that every emotion and attitude we have sits as a 'sub' emotion or attitude under one of two main categories: love or fear.

I liked this, and I embraced this way of thinking. It's easy.

It also makes a lot of sense and, when you become aware of it and test the thinking, you'll find that it's true. It suggests that, if we're happy, for example, we're feeling the love. We see love, we feel love, we are more loving. And I don't just mean love according to the meaning we're brought up to understand. I mean love as a representative of laughter, joy, confidence, assertiveness, a healthy self-esteem, humility, contentment, satisfaction, fulfilment, bliss, happiness, forgiveness, and inner strength. Love as a representative of every good feeling we experience, every good attitude we carry around. Love as a representative of living and speaking our truth. If we're worried, embarrassed, lacking in confidence, greedy, dishonest, guilty, intimidating or intimidated, arrogant, or aggressive, we're carrying fear about something.

Love carries no weight. Happiness carries no weight. Joy, bliss, and laughter carry no weight. They are free, and they feel free. They make you feel like shouting and laughing in the wind. They make you feel that you *can*; in fact, they know you can.

Fear is heavy, debilitating, dark, a ton weight. Worry, guilt, a lack of confidence, anger, stress, arrogance – they're all versions of fear, and they're all heavy. Can you see that? If we're worried, we're fearful that something bad is going to happen. If we're feeling guilty, we're beating up on ourselves, and we're fearful that someone's thinking something negative about us. If we lack confidence, we fear that we're not living up to expectations or that others are better than we are. If we're angry, we're often venting about a heaviness we're carrying about, or we're angry because we're not comfortable with something or living our truth. We get angry that we're trapped in something we're too scared to get out of or deal with. If we're stressed, we're fearful that we're not going to get something done, or that we'll miss something, or that we've got too much to do, or that someone is looking for something from us that we're unable to give. Or some other reason. If we're displaying arrogance, we're needing to feel superior, better, or 'more', or we're putting up a shield to protect ourselves from something. All of these emotions come from some element of fear. Many of us are living in a great big cycle of fear in which one aspect triggers off another aspect, and down we go, deeper and deeper into the fear spiral. Frustration, intimidation, competition, comparison, embarrassment, anxiety, panic: there are endless fear-based emotions dragging us down.

Don't think you shouldn't ever feel fear. That's not what this section of this book is about. As humans, we have the capacity to feel a huge range of emotions, and so we should. Emotions are our messengers. They're our guidance. It's unreasonable and misguided to think that we could or should always be living with only love and glee.

♥ Treat fear as a message, and seek love.

However, it's also unreasonable to allow ourselves to accept that it's okay to live with as much fear in our lives as we do today. Fear messes you up, knocks you down, hangs you out to dry. It's a very heavy, bleak, and negative load. It should be a temporary messenger rather than a long-term resident.

The following passage is an excerpt from *Conversations with God Book 1: An Uncommon Dialogue* by Neale Donald Walsch[5]. Using a few dozen words, Walsch simplifies the way we live, and in so doing illuminates the fundamental reason for our individual and worldly issues. It gives us somewhere to start, something to go on, and, hence, is incredibly empowering:

> Every human thought, and every human action, is based in either love or fear. There *is* no other human motivation, and all other ideas are but derivatives of these two. They are simply different versions – different twists on the same theme.

> Think on this deeply and you will see that it is true. This is what I have called the Sponsoring Thought. It is either a thought of love or fear. This is the thought behind the thought *behind* the thought. It is the first thought. It is prime force. It is the raw energy that drives the engine of human experience.

Walsch goes on to offer the most beautiful, humbling, and enlightening section of prose I ever remember hearing. It was poetry to my ears when I first became aware of it. I'd read it before, but it was when I was listening to an audio version of the book that, as I found myself transfixed by the clarity and ease of the description, I stopped everything I was doing, rewound the passage, found my coloured pencils, and created it in my notepad.

> Fear is the energy which contracts, closes down, draws in, runs, hides, hoards, harms. Love is the energy

which expands, opens up, sends out, stays, reveals, shares, heals. Fear wraps our bodies in clothing, love allows us to stand naked. Fear clings to and clutches all that we have, love gives all that we have away. Fear holds close, love holds dear. Fear grasps, love lets go. Fear rankles, love soothes. Fear attacks, love amends.

Every human thought, word or deed is based in one emotion or the other. You have no choice about this, because there is nothing else from which to choose.

But you have free choice about which of these to select.

Choose Not to Fear

Fear envelopes everything that is negative. Fear is like a cloud of lots of aspects of woe. Fear is an active part of our societies, our governments, our religions, our media, our families, our schools, our communities, our upbringings, and hence, too much of our lives. For generations – for centuries – we've been brought up to feel the fear. We have allowed ourselves to be compromised and controlled by the powers that be and have long forgotten we've got a choice about whether we listen to and believe in what we're being fed or not. We've long forgotten we can question things, research things, become informed, and make up our own minds.

❤ You *can* make up your own mind.

There's part of the reason I stopped going to university right there – because no essay or part of an exam was based on anything that I'd managed to discern or decipher myself. All that was expected of me was that I would regurgitate the theories we'd been fed that semester. I got marked down if I had an opinion, used the 'wrong' font, used the 'wrong' spacing, or inserted a new paragraph where the fourth-year who was marking my work thought there shouldn't be one. We're encouraged to go to university because our degree demonstrates to an employer that we can commit to something and see it through. Does it also show that employer that we're passive, submissive, and content being told what to think?

We *can* question things, research things, become informed, and make up our own minds. We *can* choose to avoid fear, listen to the message in the fear, and stand taller than fear. We *can* choose not to live in or with fear but to use it to our benefit. We live in societies that encourage debilitating behaviour, with governments and media that drip-feed us what they want us to know and that discourage us from thinking for ourselves and using our intelligence. We're taught that we have to win simply to have the chance to keep up. We can choose to hear the message in our fear and stand above it. We can choose to deal with it objectively, constructively, and in a way that serves us. That means we can choose to *accept* the message and make any necessary changes. Alternatively, we can choose to ignore the message, store it, and allow it to eat away at us and become a burden.

♥ Throw away your mantle of fear.

Think of a day in the life of you. How much negativity – I'm going to call it fear – is there around you? From the minute you get up till the minute you go to bed, how much fear-based behaviour do you come across or create? It's everywhere. Often it's driven by you yourself. Just as often, it's induced or motivated by others or by something. You don't have to look hard. On one hand, there are people putting fear into us all day every day – insurance for this, scare tactics for that, official letters written using bold and threatening wording. We're told we'd better act now so we don't miss out, or to buy this while it's on offer at a 'huge' ten per cent off. On the other hand, there are people living in fear, consumed by fear, for various and infinite reasons, who insist obliviously and without any consideration or self or social awareness, to blame the world for everything that's happening to them, making excuses and shedding their woes on innocent, unprotected bystanders.

And all too often we accept their woes instead of challenging them, encouraging them that there *is* something to live for, that life is quite beautiful and amazing.

💜 Let love blow fear away.

Think about the messages being put out there in every advert you watch or listen to. Whatever compassionate and understanding, warm and fuzzy, caring for your well-being message they seem to be portraying, they all want something from you, so they're going to find a way to scare you into submission.

Not to mention the fear that the news puts into us, that religions put into us, that television, newspapers, and magazines put into us.

Not to mention the fact that our education systems are teaching what the government dictates, which is often very little about real life.

Not to mention arriving at work every day and being drawn into whatever uninspiring behaviour is going on there.

We're all being 'dumbed down' while all of this is going on. The less we question the 'authority' and think for ourselves, the easier we are to control. The more fear we are fed, the more fearful we become and the easier we are to manipulate. The more we are spoken to as if we're toddlers – and don't notice we're being spoken to as if we're toddlers – the easier we are to condition.

And then, of course, there are all the other fear-related emotions that result from these fear-based messages.

But you and I don't need to accept any of this treatment. You and I can stand above what's going on around us and have a positive effect on what happens in our own space and within our own reach. As Gandhi said, 'Be the change you want to see in the world'. To be that change, live with love. Exchange the fear-based emotions for love-based emotions.

I realise this section may sound harsh. I've considered whether to include these words or not. They're not particularly loving words, but they are words to make you think. I want you to think about the world and the reality around you. You may be feeling a little prickly, shivery, jaggy, or uncomfortable. These may not be words you want to hear or think about. Remember they reflect my opinion. They reflect my belief. They may not reflect your opinion or belief. But I do urge you to think about what I've said and to test it for yourself. To enable positive change within, we need to be aware of what's going on outside. Without being properly aware of the realities around us – the ones that we're allowing to touch us – it's difficult to take the step into our own power and consciously manage how, if, and to what extent we choose connect with or detach from what's going on around us.

Watch the documentary film *The Cosmic Giggle*[6] when you get the chance. It's all about the human energy field and its real and perceived effects on reality, and it will help explain all of this a bit further.

💜 Step into your own power and treat fear on *your* terms.

Getting Along With Your Ego

How much nicer would life be if we weren't all trying to compete with our ego selves. Your inner being – your heart – respects you. Your inner being loves you wholly and unconditionally and wants you to shine brightly every day. Your inner self is comfortable in and with itself. Your inner self is generous to you, says kind things to you, and treats you with beauty and compassion. And you deserve all of those things. You deserve love. You deserve to feel comfortable and to receive generosity and kindness. And, you *are* beautiful and compassionate.

Yet when last did you see your inner self? When last did you even acknowledge your inner self? That person is *you*. That person is the sweet light that has already started to shine because you have offered up appreciation and embraced the energy in and around you. That person is who you really are, and for that special, beautiful, patient being inside, it's time to take some more little steps to give *you* the airspace you deserve. It's time to open up to life in the love zone rather than the fear zone. Stand up straight, own your power, and decide to live true to yourself instead of simply following the pack. You don't need unimportant material objects, consumer goods, or the pack in your life. They're not what will bring you peace. You need love, good feelings, nature, and truth.

♥ Get ready to live in the love zone.

We are ego-centred beings living in an ego-centric world.

I first learned about the ego from Don Miguel Ruiz in his book, *The Four Agreements: A Practical Guide to Personal Wisdom*[7]. I learned that actually *I* had an ego. I thought that only arrogant people had egos; I associated 'ego' with 'arrogance'. But that's not true. We all have egos. And Don Miguel Ruiz highlighted the fact that it was my ego that expected I was being talked about, judged, and condemned by others. Ruiz asked me to think about why I felt I was worthy of other people's judgements and condemnation. He asked what made me think other people had time in their day to be thinking about and talking about me.

You have an ego. I have an ego. We all have egos. It's our egos that are holding us in fear. Ego prompts our stress response, and our stress response goes way back to our early ancestors. You may have heard of the fight, flight, or freeze response. When our ancestors met with a threatening or dangerous situation, their egos instinctively sent messages to their brains, and their brains generated stress hormones so that they could protect themselves from the danger or threat. The high stress was as temporary as the threat. Once the danger passed, their fear and stress would pass.

There are still communities in the world living like that today, and we laugh at them, belittle them, and view them as inferior, priding ourselves that, in the Western world, we are better, smarter, and more intelligent.

Yet who really should be laughing? Today our egos are part of the furniture. In our Western societies, we are living almost permanently in a state of stress, surrounded by a constant and accelerating gush of doom, gloom, and fear in one form or another. And while we're in that state of stress, our egos are also permanently present. Yet our egos are no longer serving us in the way they should be, or protecting us properly. We're often ready to react to a threat before we even know if there's a threat there. In fact, our egos are *so* implanted in us that our heads tell us what threats are out there for us. We make things up! We are so highly stressed that we *invent* the danger that's going to come our way on any given day. Our definition of true danger has become so marred that we brace ourselves for the fearsome and tiresome people around us. We brace ourselves for what's going to come at us all day long, in whatever form it takes. And because of our permanent state of stress, as we've learned in the earlier chapters, we attract more and more stress.

There really is no *true* danger in most of our days. And if there is, and we are genuinely living with such high stress, then we need to be looking at what that danger is and taking steps to either diminish it or remove it from our lives. This may require some professional counselling or a particular form of expertise.

The ego has its place; we just need to keep it in its place. It has its moments, but rarely are we in the state of emergency our ego and our stress hormones were designed for. That's why we need to receive our ego as a messenger and remain objective and empowered. Just as we should tread cautiously when we read the content of a newspaper, so we should tread cautiously in how seriously we take our egos.

As individuals, as communities, as nations, we really need to reduce the level and state of fear in which we're living. It doesn't need to be the way it is.

💙 Thank your ego for bringing you the message.

You Have Been Taught to Live in Fear

I'd like to share another important passage from *Conversations with God Book 1: An Uncommon Dialogue* by Neale Donald Walsch.

> You have been taught to live in fear. You have been told about the survival of the fittest and the victory of the strongest and the success of the cleverest. Precious little is said about the glory of the most loving. And so you strive to be the fittest, the strongest, the cleverest – in one way or another – and if you see yourself as something less than this in any situation, you fear loss, for you have been told that to be less is to lose.[8]

The Amygdala: Fear Centre of the Brain

Here's a brain fact: The amygdala is the part of your brain associated with your fight, flight, or freeze response; hence, it is the part of your brain that stimulates your stress, fear, and anxiety emotions and behaviours.

Here's something *huge*: The amygdala responds quicker than your conscious mind to any available triggers.

Did you follow that? The amygdala responds *quicker* than your conscious mind to any available triggers!

No wonder it's so hard to feel positive emotions! We've been brought up in a fear-based world, so we habitually live in and expect the fear-based response. What makes it doubly and even more excruciatingly difficult to feel positive emotions is that the amygdala kicks in as soon as there's the slightest tremor of anything related to fear!

That's why, as soon as you feel a worry thought, or a guilt thought, or a negative thought, or some judgemental thought about yourself or somebody else – as soon as you feel anything negative about to take hold in your head – it's important to do everything you can to turn that negative into a positive.

Don't give in to it. Stay in your power.

Find ways to *make* your mind think about something happy, or go and do something that will make you smile, laugh, or feel joy.

Breathe deeply (see Part Two for details) and focus sincerely on generating a feeling associated with something, somebody, or a situation you love or that brings you peace. Dr David Hamilton, a former pharmaceutical industry chemist, is now a researcher and author of many books, including *How Your Mind Can Heal Your Body* and *Why Kindness Is Good For You*. Dr Hamilton advises that the brain can't tell the difference between whether you're actually doing something or just thinking about it. So, if you think of – and *feel* – being with someone you love, or in a place that you love, your body reacts in the same way it would if you were in that situation.

HeartMath® Institute, an organisation dedicated to helping people connect their hearts and minds, also encourages carrying out the steps I've just outlined. They call it their Quick Coherence® Technique and they recommend it to help restore equilibrium and stop negative thoughts from depleting your energy and turning into something they shouldn't: 'Find a feeling of ease and inner harmony that's reflected in more balanced heart rhythms.'[9]

Stop that stress response. Stop it!

Having said all that, once you pay attention to your feelings, your intuition, your inner being, you'll 'hear', or *feel*, your inner self over your subconscious thought because, remember, your inner self answers your question before you've even finished asking it.

Oh what a complex and amazing being you are. You just need to seize your power and turn some things around.

❤ *You* are a beautiful complex being, and *you* have the power.

Doodle, Scribble, Create!

Doodle, scribble, create at least five things that make you laugh, make you happy, and bring you joy in some way. Carry this with you so that you can use it to catch a negative thought before it takes hold. Don't feed your amygdala — have a list of happy thoughts handy so that you can stop that stress reaction before it starts.

Take control, my friend, and know you can.
This is your amazing adventure!

Love: Live it, Love it, Be it

I've just written a few pages on demonstrating fear. I'm not going to write pages on demonstrating love. Love, joy, and happiness are emotions we can recognise much more easily than many of the conditioned, fear-based behaviours we enact without realising we're doing so. We're so used to living without a whole lot of love-based emotions and behaviours in our lives that they stand out when we change our behaviours and implant them in our days.

However, they can be a little difficult to generate at first, since we've spent so long living with the imbalance brought on by too much fear.

As I mentioned earlier, love is the polar opposite of fear. And, if fear is everything negative, then love is everything positive. You know love when you 'see' it. This whole book is about feeling it, seeing it, applying it, expressing it, living it, recognising it, and being it. Right now, you know love when you see it in its more obvious forms – the forms you've been brought up to recognise as being evidence of love.

Now I'd like you to acknowledge love in all its splendour, within you and around you and in the purest form of honest, authentic, peaceful, assertive behaviour.

Love looks and feels like joy, peace, harmony, optimism, positivity, empathy, kindness, generosity, forgiveness, confidence, graciousness, assertiveness, acceptance, belief, honesty, faith, trust, happiness, laughter, grace, compassion, truth, laughter, hope, smiles, hugs, dreams, and good intentions.

> Love is within man. It is not imported from the outside.
> It is not a commodity to be purchased when we go to the markets.
> It is there as the fragrance of life. It is inside everyone.[10]
> Osho

I'd love for you to open up to finding ways of living more love. Anger hardens our arteries. Love and compassionate thoughts don't; they widen our blood vessels, which is a good thing. Dr David Hamilton talks about 'emotional contagion': you feel happy being around happy people; you feel stressed being around stressed people. He also supports the view that just thinking of a thing or a person that you love generates the hormone oxytocin, and oxytocin sweeps free radicals and inflammation out of our blood streams. Free radicals aren't as joyous as they perhaps sound; they're unstable atoms or groups of atoms in your body that you don't want to be there.

I'd like you to focus on bringing more loving feelings and gradually more loving, accountable people into your life. The only way you can generate more love in your life is to consciously focus on what you're allowing to go on in your head. And the way you can regulate what you're allowing to go on in your head is to pay attention to and manage the ego aspects of your life. Think about where you can turn your choices around. You can choose to watch and read media that feeds you love and good feelings; they do exist, and you don't have to look far to find them. You can choose to read material that encourages you to be *you,* that advocates being yourself and being happy in and with your world. You can choose to pursue activities that bring you joy and energy and make you feel alive. You can choose to spend time with people who energise and empower you and bring you to life. Your energy is *you*; protect it.

Decide today to make the rest of your life a sound exercise in love, harmony, authenticity, and peace.

♥ Choose love; it's good for you.

Listen to the Message in the Fear, and Feel the Love

As I've said, fear does have a place in our lives. We are emotional beings, and our feelings can't all be one sided. We wouldn't be normal – we wouldn't be human – if we felt only love. We'd have no opportunity to be real, and we wouldn't expand or become enriched, especially not in the world we live in right now, if we felt only love. Without fear in our lives, we wouldn't have the challenge or opportunity to grow or advance. Approached correctly, with confidence, strength, and a healthy self-esteem, fear can egg us on, push us to the next stage, take us to a place of empowerment we've never experienced before. Fear can take us onwards and upwards if we listen to its messages, consider them objectively, act constructively, and don't allow the emotion to consume us.

At the moment, we've mostly just got the balance and the focus all wrong. We've got everything back to front. Feelings of fear and negativity should be temporary visitors, not lodgers who outstay their welcome. We should embrace fear and negativity when they come a-calling, not meet them with a sinking heart believing straight away that they've won and that they're here for the duration. They'll squat for as long as we allow them to.

I once worked in a place where I was surrounded by a lot of anger, some of it directed at me. For a while, that negative emotion came at me hard and fast, and I got bogged down taking it personally. I got to the stage where I was no longer able to see it rationally. Once I realised what was going on, I made a conscious decision to stop and look at what everybody was actually angry about. I realised, acknowledged, and accepted that none of the anger was anything to do with anything I had done or been involved in.

This observation and realisation helped me to make the choice to stop taking the anger personally and to stop allowing other people's fear to flatten me. By looking closely at what was going on, I acknowledged that their anger was related to 'events before my time' and that none of what the anger was about could be reasonably attributed to me. I also acknowledged that none of the sources of the anger actually knew me, so it couldn't be personal. I just happened to be in the firing line. Using a combination of many of the tips I'm giving you in this book, I made myself step back and stop taking people's venting personally. I made myself read e-mails objectively and without emotion, and I started consciously picturing myself reacting calmly and with understanding to e-mails and receiving more thank you e-mails and more generous e-mails in my in box.

♥ Look inside to improve what's going on the outside.

In Part Two, I will talk about the power of setting intentions. As soon as I stopped taking people's anger personally, a lot of it either diminished or I was able to view it differently, often just accepting their anger as something they had to work on and something that was theirs rather than mine. Other people's anger wasn't (and isn't) something I could actually do anything about other than to progress their piece of work honestly, objectively, and with open communication. When I stopped taking things personally and carried on assertively and impartially with the job I was doing, people calmed down, saw I was well intended and did what I said I was going to do, and we were able to communicate factually, objectively, and constructively and achieve so very much more than we did when we were sitting in a place of fear.

What's more, I came in one Monday morning to half a dozen e-mails that all started with 'thank you'.

You really *can* turn your world around.

Large or small, long term or short term, major or minor, any fear-based emotion is your constructive guidance. It's telling you that there's something you need to deal with, that this situation should be temporary. It's telling you that you can learn from the experience, and you can try to make sure fear doesn't reoccur in relation to this particular situation. As you progress and get more used to listening to what's inside, you'll welcome these messages as indications and guidance. They'll help you create good feelings and stop getting stuck in bad ones – if you're open and allow them to.

> The ego only understands the language of taking; the language of giving is love.[11]
> Osho

Doodle, Scribble, Create!

Write down one fear-based emotion you feel in your life regularly.

For example, do you wake up every morning worrying? Have you been feeling guilty for months over something you said or did that you can't change? Do you feel anxious about going to work, or somewhere else? Do you doubt yourself or are you carrying around something unsaid? Do you feel judged, intimidated, in competition, or angry about a certain person or thing? Anything that's giving you a bad feeling is related to fear, so pick something and just write it down. Don't scribble, doodle, and create it because that'll just enhance it and validate it.

We're going to come back to this feeling later in the book. For the time being, though, consider why you're feeling this feeling. Establish your truth about the feeling and situation. The feeling will give you a message if you allow it to. This is a good opportunity to start listening with your heart and to start being receptive to what your feelings are telling you — whether you like the message or not.

Is the feeling telling you that something in your life needs to change? Be honest with yourself. If it does, good! The feeling is an indicator.

And now, open your heart and start to exercise love. Doodle, scribble, create some initial steps you might be able to take to change this feeling and move on from it. We're not expecting life-changing activity at this stage, but knowing what you've read so far, and with the focus and time out to consider what's going on, now is a good time to review how you can turn this feeling into a neutral or better feeling. What are you going to do or change in your days to exercise more love, more happiness, more joy? Think about the law of attraction. Think about energy and clear flow. Think about choices and free will. Think about appreciation, love, and being thankful. Let your imagination run. Let your creativity free. Don't try. Just let yourself go with this. There could be something in your doodles. It's time for you to break free from this constant feeling of fear.

Spirituality versus Religion

I HAD ALMOST DEFINITELY DECIDED NOT to include a section such as this one in this book in case it was too much too soon. However, I've received a few signs recently that indicate I should not leave it out.

Spirituality is a broad concept that means different things to so many of us. Indeed, sometimes we can't really define it in our own heads. Often we link it purely to religion.

At the time of writing, I've described spirituality on my website in the following way:

- Looking inside instead of out. Shining your own light. Living your truth. Being yourself.
- Listening to you – to your heart, your intuition, your own depth. Developing a higher level of awareness of consciousness. Becoming comfortable with who you are, not who you've been conditioned to become. Reviewing your relationship with yourself, your body, the world around you. Reconsidering your relationship with your day, your future, your past.
- Thickening your pre-frontal cortex. Consciously managing your thoughts before they reach your amygdala. Showing your ego who's boss. Being choosy about who and what guides you. Being responsible, being your own leader, blaming no one. Achieving unconditional self-acceptance and love.

- Connecting with nature – breathing, inhaling, soaking up life. Feeling happy, confident, and content being *you*. Being able just to *be*.

Spirituality means connecting back to who you really are. Reclaiming *you*. Trusting and following your intuition, your inner guidance. I believe we were all born as spiritual beings. To me, spirituality means being true to yourself; believing in yourself; having confidence in your innermost feelings; and living with love, compassion, care, appreciation, and acceptance.

God

When my massage therapist first offered to lend me Neale Donald Walsch's book, *Conversations with God Book 1: An Uncommon Dialogue*, I shied away from the offer a little and replied that I 'wasn't really religious'. Vanessa told me it wasn't a religious book and that she felt, from the topics and the depth of conversations we'd shared, it was something I would enjoy.

And she was right. At the time, I felt a little embarrassed at my closed-minded reaction to Vanessa, but in hindsight, I also realise that, for so many years, I allowed myself to remain scared and uncomfortable about anything related to the realm of religion because I didn't understand or know enough about it. We are brought up to believe certain things, and sometimes it takes a lifetime to challenge our beliefs and work things out for ourselves. For me, it took a move to Australia when I was twenty-five to realise that the world didn't fall apart if you didn't send everybody you'd ever met in your whole life a Christmas card. For a period of time I stopped sending Christmas cards, and now I've found a balance and send them – and receive them – as thoughtful, loving gestures rather than obligations or expectations.

Anyway, the book. I'd always been open to learning new things, and although Vanessa's offer seemed a little confronting, the opportunity for learning was being handed to me on a plate. Vanessa knew me better than I knew myself back then during the years when she was in my life. She was a true guide for me at the time.

Conversations with God Book 1: An Uncommon Dialogue started answering questions for me, and encouraged me to open my mind more and more to what could be out there, what our universal truth really is, and what more we know that we don't hear about through 'accepted' mainstream sources. The *Conversations with God* series continues to provide me with an abundance of answers, guidance, and reminders. Indeed, I find the books make *so* much sense and offer a clear explanation of precisely why humanity has gone so off track.

♥ God, the universe, energy, source – it's all love.

My current understanding and belief is that God is everywhere. And just as it is with the definition of spirituality, I've learned that the definition of God is different for many people too. Further, I understand that people of the Christian faith – maybe of all faiths – believe that everyone has a personal relationship with God, which, by its very nature, makes God different for everyone.

God is essentially the universe I talked about in Part One. God is sometimes referred to as the universe, the source, Allah, all that is, the creator, or source energy. Just the other day I heard God referred to as light energy. The name isn't really important. I usually talk about the universe. A special friend of mine says 'up there where all the souls are'. Whatever it is that's out there is our power. We are connected to it, and it is working with us to create our intentions. It's a non-physical energy that is neither male nor female, and it is there to offer us pure love and guidance and support. God was not created by a religious group; God existed before religious groups formed.

Religion

I have not delved deeply into many religions. As my heart, my mind, and my eyes have opened, and I've questioned and investigated what I was brought up with – indeed what we are all brought up with, as there's no getting away from the governing effect that religion and religious beliefs have on our communities, our countries, our whole world – I've found my own path leads to spirituality. For me, spirituality surpasses each and every religion.

Spirituality is what we are. Religion is what we've been taught. For me, it's as simple as that. Spirituality is inherent in us; religion is just something we've learnt. Spirituality is depth; religion is surface deep. Spirituality has existed since the universe began; religion is new and man-made.

Spirituality is part of religion, but religion is not part of spirituality. Spirituality can stand alone; religion is selective about its use of and reference to spirituality.

To me, spirituality breeds love, and religion breeds fear. Just as does every other aspect of our lives as human beings, religion encourages fear – fear that we should feel condemned by God and expect to be punished and/or forgiven for sins and wrong doings. Yet who should be the judge of what is sin and what is wrong? Indeed, even in our societies the view on that changes by decade or generation. If God gave us free will, how can anything actually be *wrong*? Shouldn't that mean we're here to make our own choices, to try things, to work it all out for ourselves? Aren't we here to find the difference between what feels good and what doesn't, how love feels and how fear feels and then act accordingly? Collectively, at a worldwide level, we've chosen fear. And the law of attraction ensures that the more fear we generate, the more fear we'll generate.

> ♥ Love is all around you; you just need to open your heart to receive.

I have also realised that people can be religious, but that doesn't mean they're spiritual. There are many people who attend religious services and go to buildings of religion for reasons beyond my understanding.

If more of us can live in and with love, peace, kindness, compassion, and generosity, we can surely hope that some of those who live only in and with their egos may feel the glimmer of their own lights shining inside and choose to come along with us.

You're a Spiritual Being

Whatever your own thoughts and religious beliefs, you are a spiritual and an empowered being.

Spirituality is about you shining your light. It's about you living true to yourself, your beliefs, and your own universal source – or God – that helps you to listen to your intuition, live your truth, and sing your song. It's about you being guided by your feelings and your heart. You were born spiritual; your spirituality is still inside. Your spirituality *is* your shining light. You were an Olympic torch when you were born; now you've got a little match alight inside. We want your torch high and bright and alight and guiding your way.

It's taken me over thirty years to get to the point where I can put some sort of structure around what I now know and believe about spirituality and religion. I don't claim to be an expert; neither do I presume to suggest to you what you should think. Spirituality is in religion, but you can be – and are – a highly spiritual being without the need to have any link to or interest in any religion. This discussion can be confronting, challenging, and difficult. Yet it can also be very freeing and empowering. Thinking differently about something you've been brought up to believe and have always believed – or at the very least have not questioned – can significantly change your life.

God, the universe, all that is, source – it's all spiritual. It is pure, perfect energy that exists above, beyond, and without religion.

You too are that pure perfect energy.

💜 Spirituality is pure.

Doodle, Scribble, Create!

Doodle, scribble, create whatever you like here now that you have read the section on 'Spirituality versus Religion'. It can be a heavy topic and one that can be confronting and personal, as it is for me. Hence, I am leaving you with no guidance other than your own.

Go with your Olympic torch here, and let your intuition flow.

PART TWO

What Else is True?

*W*hat Else is True?

YOU ARE WORTHY!

You are capable!

You can reach the sky!

Reach high, earth child. You are more than you have ever imagined!

> Absolutely we are *not* what we have been told and I can tell you absolutely that we are more than we have ever, ever imagined.

These words were spoken by Gregg Braden to Greg Sherwood during their conversation on Braden's area of expertise, *The Uncharted Heart: The New Discoveries in Science*, at the May 2016 Hay House World Summit.

So 'what else is true' is that you are *not* what you have been told you are, and you are much more than you have ever imagined. I hope that, by the end of Part One, you got a sense of that. And I pray that by now you are getting a sense of your potential and some realisation that your level of capability is so much more than you've ever allowed yourself to consider.

Part One dealt with what is known and understood of our world today – what *is*. You can research everything in Part One and dig deeper into areas that resonate with you or that you're curious to know more about. The universe is one amazing generator that is waiting to work with you as you create the next part of your life's adventure.

Part Two is all about you. It is about helping you to see, appreciate, and accept how powerful you are. We all are! We've had our power beaten out of us over the years. We've been conditioned towards fear and negativity, and it's time for us to choose empowerment, stand tall, and generate more love, ease, happiness, and compassion for ourselves.

♥ You are more than you know. Set yourself free.

Part Two shares tips, techniques, and suggestions that I've tried, and most of which I live with continuing improvement. As I tried different things and realised they made a difference, I began to make ways to embed them into my life. Gradually, changes you make become habits, which we all know from the many bad ones we have means that we do things without having to think about them.

Some of the tips may be confronting, and you may feel uncomfortable about some of them. Change doesn't come easily or without effort, focus, and commitment. Being open is one of the main things I talk about in Part Two. Unless you open your heart and mind to possibility and hope, you won't change anything.

Yet, from making even the smallest changes, you grow in subtle enriching ways. And from the most difficult or challenging experiences, you grow in the biggest, most profound ways. The changes you're invited to consider making here are *inside* you and will help you let your sun shine!

You Are and You Can

You are what's inside. Your light's still there. The person who was born all those years ago is still inside your soul. And we're going to remind you of who and what that is. You are the beauty and perfection that's inside.

You are and you *can*. You *can* do everything I've done, and more, to make changes to the way you feel inside. And, ironically, you do that by paying attention to the way you feel inside.

Remember, your feelings are indicators. We're not looking at achieving life-long continuity of only good feelings; we're looking at becoming more aware of our feelings and generating good ones more often than bad. The bad ones are messages, though; you want them. They tell you things.

💜 Put your effort into *you*.

You *can* do many things. Part of making any change is believing in yourself. I want you to hold your hands high and shout to the sky because you really can believe in yourself. Now is the time to look at your circle of friends, your networks and acquaintances, and the environments in which you participate, because if these don't encourage and support you, if your people and your environments are discouraging, negative, and draining, they won't serve you. You might consider dropping them as you adopt new philosophies. Denise Linn, in her *Soul Coaching*® book, talks about reducing zappers and increasing juicers. We'll talk more about what's serving you and what's not throughout the course of Part Two, but think about the extent to which a less-than-supportive circle of acquaintances might be aiding your negativity – or zapping you – and pay attention to what you read, listen to, and say. 'Be impeccable with your word' as Don Miguel Ruiz says in his book, *The Four Agreements: A Practical Guide to Personal Wisdom*.[12] Protect your senses and be choosy about what's allowed in and what you give out.

💜 Be bold and brazen in your encouragement of *you*.

Lesley MacCulloch

Imagine your true self – your inner being – as your very best and unconditionally loving friend. Motivate your friend openly, inspire it with joy, nurture it, encourage it, reassure it, and tell it you love it. Be bold and brazen in your encouragement of it, and show it patience and compassion along the way. It is *you*. Don't let *you* down any longer by continuing to listen only to your head and the external sources in your life. Consider that you have a responsibility to your true self (now you know it's still in there) to live your light, to feel good. Why would you want *you* to feel unhappy, to laugh rarely, to feel sadness, to struggle and experience hardship? Think of *you* as you do your sons and daughters. Think of *you* as you do your very best friends, as you do the ones you love. Why are *you* a lesser being?

You are worthy of your love, your care, your friendship, your compliments, your kindness, your encouragement, your patience, your laughter, and your happy chitchat. You *can* put just as much – more! – energy into making yourself happy as you do in trying to make other people happy.

Write down these statements and as you write them say them aloud:

I am perfect and I am equal to my fellow human beings.

I am worthy of my love, my care, my friendship, my compliments, my kindness, my encouragement, my patience, my laughter, and my happy chitchat.

I put more energy into making myself happy than I do into making other people happy.

Challenge your beliefs about yourself. By doing that, you can address what's going on and create positive and *true* beliefs rather than living with stuff you've been told or have conditioned yourself to believe.

Make yourself happy and you will bring others along your feel-good path with you anyway. Just as negativity is contagious and toxic, so is positivity energising and powerful.

> People get confused in this conversation cause they'll say 'Well I'm not a murderer or I'm not a rapist' but I would say, find out what kind of person would be a murderer, what kind of person would be a rapist. Those are the kind of questions that we must ask ourselves cause maybe a rapist would be somebody who's wounded or sick. We *all* have a wounded part of ourselves, we all have a sick part of ourselves, we all have a twisted part of ourselves, and even though we'd like to fit in to the ego's ideal of being 'a perfect human being', we're not; we're all that there is. And when we can open our hearts and have compassion for the part of us that might murder, we have no idea if we're capable of that … but maybe, maybe in the right or wrong circumstances we are all capable of anything: the most beautiful, glorious act of greatness and what we would consider one of the most horrible crimes against humanity. And when we embrace all of ourselves knowing that we're both human and that we are divine, well voila, all of a sudden you have a whole human being and what you feel is one-ness.[13]
> Debbie Ford in James F Twyman's film
> *The Moses Code*

Υou Are ...

WHEN DID ANYONE, INCLUDING YOURSELF, LAST tell you that you're just right the way you are?

Okay, now answer truthfully – what *exactly* was your reaction to that first line, to that question? Did any of it go along the lines of 'Hmph, not in a long time' or 'Well, I'm not'.

You would probably be the last person to tell yourself that you're just right the way you are.

Yet, believe me, you are just right the way you are. You have everything in you to be the best, the nicest, the warmest, the happiest of that person, and it's time for you to get used to that.

I'm going to say that again: You have everything in you to be the best, the nicest, the warmest, the happiest of that person.

And now, go on, tell me why you haven't got everything in you. Go on. In fact, write it here:

_____

_____

_____

How much of what you wrote above relates to other people and circumstances that are out of your own power or control?

My guess is that, up there on those three lines, are thoughts like 'maybe I would be if I didn't have this job, if it wasn't for my daughter, if it wasn't for my boss, colleague, teacher, brother, sister, son, friend, car, if it wasn't for the state of my house, my body, my income, my debt, the council, the weather.'

(My mum just added in 'my age'.)

I wonder if any of you actually wrote something like 'maybe I would be if I didn't have this ego, these bad feelings inside me, this head that keeps telling me otherwise, this past that I allow to haunt me. Maybe I would be if I could better deal with the job I have, my daughter, my boss, my colleague, my teacher, brother, sister. Maybe I would be if I could care less about the state of my house, my body, my income, my debt, the weather – my age.'

Can you see the difference between these two paragraphs? Can you *feel* the difference between these two paragraphs? Why do they feel different?

The first paragraph focuses on external sources that you can't do anything about. The first paragraph focuses on defeat and allows everything external to control how you're feeling and what you're thinking about yourself.

The second paragraph focuses on internal sources and accountability, and offers the opportunity of empowerment, forgiveness, and assertiveness. The second paragraph reminds you that it's *you* who can change all that. 'Maybe I would and could be the nicest warmest happiest version of myself if, inwardly, I dealt with the things that aren't working for me in my life and allowed others to take responsibility for themselves.' 'Maybe I would and could be the nicest warmest happiest version of myself if I could forgive myself for things in my past that I'm not proud of. The past is the past. It built my character, helped me to realise my values and find my truth. It is something I give thanks for. I love who I am and I live for today.'

You can't change your past – and remember, everybody has a past, so don't let anyone, including yourself, beat you up about yours. Regrets, guilt, and worries will weigh you down and hold you back for your whole life if you let them, and what a waste that would be! Your ego will constantly inject you with emotional pain, whereas your heart – *you* – will help you to detach, heal, and move on. When you seek within, you will find forgiveness, acceptance, and self-respect.

Likewise, you can't change other people. You can't take responsibility for the way others think, believe, or act. As soon as you let go of that and accept that others also have the will and the power to make their own choices, you will feel a weight lifting. This doesn't mean you don't care about other people; it means you accept that they, like you, have choices.

It is also worth remembering that, as you look inside, others will continue looking externally and judging. Hence, not only will you listen to *you*, but by virtue of that, you will question some of the people in your life and whether you want them there or not. But because you are listening to *you* – to your own truth – you will also find the confidence and strength to act on the answers you're getting to those questions.

As I was encouraged by my wonderful husband to be myself and to appreciate that self, and as I worked through Denise Linn's *Soul Coaching®* book, I actually started to realise this for myself. During a guided meditation in my Reiki 1 course, I was taken to a bridge and encouraged to look into the water. As I looked over the little wall of the bridge into the water I found myself saying, 'You're beautiful!'

I had a twinkle in my eye. The meditation soon asked me what I'd thought or said when I looked over into the water and was focussed a little on turning that around if necessary.

My point here is that, first, I wasn't prompted to think or say anything as I looked into the water. When you're meditating, your mind just goes with the flow in ways you don't allow it to when you're focusing it on everyday things. But what was resounding here was the fact that I'd told myself voluntarily, immediately, and without a conscious thought or prompt, that I was beautiful. I nearly laughed out loud, and if I'd been in a room on my own I probably would have. As it was, I knew I had a great big grin on my face as I realised that I had finally come to a place where I was happy with myself.

This is only a tiny part of the reason that meditation helps you to stay grounded and allows your inner self to be heard.

I continue to grow in varied and sometimes diverse ways. I've tried new things and I've opened myself up to possibility as I never had before. I'm excited. I'm listening to *me*, and I'm treating me kindly. I'm encouraging myself and finding ways to empower myself.

But to everybody around me, I still look the same, and I'm still me.

♥ Only *you* know what feels right for you.

That's why I really do make the point that you already are just as you should be. It's what's inside that will enable you to take on what's next, to feel renewed and natural, and to take steps forward, upward, and towards being the person you want to be and the person you are inside. It's what's inside that will tell you when something is right.

I mentioned earlier that my friend, Heather, sings 'This little light of mine, I'm going to let it shine ...' – a beautiful reminder to listen to the light inside that's been in there our whole lives. I sing 'I am what I am.'

So let's go on to have a look at just what and why you are.

You Are Perfect

That's what you are. Go and look yourself in the eye in the mirror and tell yourself that. And before you choke, get used to this. This isn't the last time we'll do this. That mirror is your friend, and it's only because you read and listen to sources that don't serve you that you have been led to believe otherwise. We're going to be doing a lot of looking yourself in the eye with the mirror so this is a good time to have a small one close by.

'I am perfect as I am.' Go on, do it. Go now. 'I am perfect as I am.' Say it. Say 'hi' and smile and *feel* what this feels like. Feel it inside, not in your head. Introduce yourself as your new friend. 'I am perfect as I am, and I love myself for that.' Throw your arms to the sky, reach with your fingertips, and tell the world you are perfect as you are.

Yes, you will feel self-conscious, and yes, your head will probably be telling you that you're stupid. Your head is also likely to tell you that you're not perfect. But now is the time to show your ego and your head who's boss and that you're ready to start fighting back. No longer are you going to allow your ego to knock you down and keep you down; *you* are coming back to life, and *it* won't like it. It won't like it at all. *You* are finally going to be living in your own power and not that of your ego.

I want to keep saying this – you're perfect as you are. Your exercise here is to keep saying this. Keep coming back to this. I can't write a book in which I just keep saying the same things all the time, but this is important stuff here, and you need to sit up and pay attention.

Please, please, please find a way to make sure that you tell yourself this *and* that you do everything you can to *feel* it. Even just start by standing at the mirror and smiling at yourself. Say hello, good morning, hi and smile. Please, please, please find a way to listen to this and allow yourself to think that there might be something in it. I'm not asking for full belief instantly; I'm asking you to please consider that this might help you to accept, be happy with, and love yourself the way you are. The only reason you don't feel this way at the moment is that, as you were growing up, everybody else told you – or at least gave you the subliminal message – that you weren't perfect. At that point in time, you weren't aware enough of your conscious thought, your feelings, and your intuition to be able to question them, fend them off, and stick up for yourself. Eventually you started believing it and saying the same thing to yourself as you muddled along living your life. That is why you're now beating yourself up for the way you look, the things you've done or not done, the life you've led, and everything you believe you are or are not.

What we're doing now isn't new; it's just undoing years and years of conditioning. *You* are your best friend. We're introducing you to your best friend in the whole world – ever.

We *can* undo those years of conditioning. You are perfect as you are. Become your truest and most unconditional friend. Love that pimple, love that blemish, love your beautiful freckles, love your red hair, love your ears, love your nose, love your mole, love your neck, love your eyes, your eyebrows, your lips, your hips, your knees. Every part of you, every scar, every *imperfection*, makes *you* the unique and *perfect* individual you are. If there are bits you'd like to change, be objective about what bits they are and whether changing them will help your health or your ego. Be quite particular about the parts of yourself you'd like to change and your reasons for any changes you feel you'd like to make. Don't consider changing anything for ego-centred reasons; change *only* for you and for your health. I think I'm stuck with cellulite after years of whatever adverse – or normal – everyday kind of living brings on cellulite. I can now look at the tops of my legs with acceptance and kindness as they're a part of *me*. Cellulite is not who I am inside; neither does it affect the person I am inside – unless I listen to my head, or the media, both of which could convince me to allow it to dim my light.

Love or at least accept that past – those experiences, those less-than-proud moments you have in your history in this life. Everybody has them to one degree or another. Consider them constructively, and take this opportunity to leave them behind. They are not you. You don't have to live them. Grant yourself freedom from the claws of your past. Thank your past experiences for the lessons they brought you. Remembering your connection to the bigger, broader universe can help bring back your perspective. Look into different ways to forgive, detach, and move yourself on, emotionally, from the weight you've been carrying around.

Knowing *you* and knowing that you are finally there for you, just inside the mirror, can also help you to find perspective and remember there's a far bigger picture than the one your ego allows you to see every day.

You are perfect as you are. Keep that mirror close by.

💜 Look yourself in the eye and get to know *you*.

Doodle, Scribble, Create!

'I am perfect as I am!'

Stand in front of your new friend, the mirror, and smile at you. Look you in the eye and introduce yourself. You might even want to let yourself know you're on a changing journey and that you realise you've not been listening to you very much for a while. Thank you for having been there and acknowledge that your light is inside.

Take some time doing that, and then, if you can, sit down and doodle this exercise in front of a mirror.

That's all I want you to do here. Doodle, scribble, create loads of smiles, greetings and positive affirmations that you are fine and right the way you are, that what's inside is your truth, and that you're finally in a position to be able to listen and shine.

Allow yourself as long as it takes for you to believe there might actually be something in this. And then be prepared to come back again and again and again. Yes, it can be powerful, and you may find you feel a bit overcome. It's beautiful and deeply reassuring getting to know you and realising you're not alone.

Lesley MacCulloch

You Are Beautiful

That's what you are. Beautiful. So, let's do all of the above, all over again!

You should still have the mirror close to you, so do exactly the same thing again, this time telling yourself that you're beautiful and allowing yourself to *feel* beautiful. In fact, tie the two concepts together: I am perfect, and I am beautiful.

Yes, this is repetitive, and I make no apology for that. Much of the change you're going to be making is going to be made only when you practise repetition of positive action and activity in your day. That's how you got to where you are now, in the mindset you're in now – through repetition of negative action and activity and through negative validation and constant pressure.

Life is so much sunnier and lighter when you apply repetition of *positive, loving, accepting* energy and activity to your day. And because you've been living through your head, you haven't allowed yourself to *feel* beautiful. You *are* beautiful and always have been beautiful. You are a beautiful person. You are a light, a shining light.

❤ Unique, perfect, beautiful – *you.*

Beauty is inside. Beauty isn't about what you look like or whether you're acceptable in the eyes of the gossip magazine. Beauty is about *you* being beautiful. Beauty is about being caring, loving, compassionate, generous, appreciative, encouraging, gracious, and humble. If you want to take beauty to the outside, beauty is that piece of cellulite, that bald patch, that bit of flab, that pimple, that natural hair colour, that wrinkle, that whisker, that missing finger, that dodgy leg, that face of yours, that black bruised toenail (okay, that one was for me).

We are brought up to believe that the way we look matters, which is quite ridiculous given we can't do a thing about the way we look. How on earth can we judge others for the way they look or the colour they are when they were born to look and evolve that way? Equally how can we be judged? We can't do anything about whether others are going to judge us or not, but we *can* stop our own judgements and we *can* manage how we act and react to and within our judging society.

Hear it now. It doesn't matter what you look like; neither does it matter what others look like. We can't make fair judgements about people based on what they look like; neither can they about us. We do it to others, and of course we're going to get that back. As a society, we have made beauty external. It's just another external factor that we allow to dictate our lives. Beauty is what you *are*, not what you look like. Beauty is what you *do*, not whether you meet the condemning criteria of our society's portrayal of beautiful or perfect.

Beauty is deep, internal, inherent, inside. Beauty is joy. Beautiful is what you already are, and it helps you to shine your light. Feed yourself beautiful thoughts, tell yourself beautiful things – eye to eye. As you get better at that you will *feel* beautiful inside.

> There are approximately seven billion people exist on this Earth now. I think there is one common standard we share although our skin colours, languages, religious beliefs may be different. I think that is the standard of 'beauty'.[14]
> Dr Masaru Emoto

Doodle, Scribble, Create!

'I am beautiful, and I was born beautiful.'

Treat this exercise a lot like the last one. Treat beauty in the same way as you treated perfection. Doodle it, scribble it, and allow yourself to recreate it in your own life.

As you create your own beauty on this page, feel your beauty, your love, your uniqueness, your generosity, your acceptance of you. Feel you are a beautiful part of our world.

You are those things. Nothing else has to be said. You now just have to believe in yourself, have faith and patience, and be consistent with the conversations you have with yourself.

You Are Human

That's what you are. That's what we all are. That's what I mentioned a few pages ago in the 'You Are Perfect' section. And as humans, individually and collectively, we've been our own worst enemies for years. Know that everything you are is good. Know that everything you are is okay.

That doesn't mean every 'bad' thing you've done or said is 'good'. It doesn't mean you haven't ever done anything you're not proud of. It doesn't mean that, if you did or said something that was a disservice to someone yesterday or this morning or ten years ago, that it's okay.

What it does mean, though, is that whatever you've done is done; whatever you said has been said. It does mean that *you* – you inside – can learn from your experiences and grow in your awareness, wisdom, and enrichment from every experience you've ever had. We can't change things we've said or done, but we can consider what we've said and why we said those things and address the reasons that prompted us to carry out those behaviours, to take those actions. We can seek to apologise to others and to amend our ways; we can search inside to understand and grant ourselves forgiveness, but we can't turn back the clock. And that's where we get stuck. We get stuck in the past. We live with regret, guilt, sadness, and insecurity instead of addressing the occurrences and associated emotions so we can accept them, grow from them, detach from them, and move on from them.

Know that there is help, support, and understanding here and around you. We're at a time in humanity where things are changing. There is much research being carried out. A great deal of new evidence is being found about the connection and interaction between the brain and the heart, and also about the connection between our own level of consciousness and humanity's collective level of consciousness. We are human, and we've done and we continue to do what we were brought up to do. We have been led by science, religion, bureaucracy, and authority. We've even been led by authorities within authorities. We've often got confused in our ever-changing world about what's 'right' and 'wrong', what's 'acceptable' and what's not, because what used to be 'right' is now 'wrong' and vice versa. We try so hard to be what we 'should' be, but that often conflicts with the sparkles we have inside and our often-well-hidden but no-less-existing values. As a result, we act in ways we're not even sure we understand ourselves. We long to know ourselves, to feel empowered, and to live true to ourselves, yet we're so conditioned to our external world that we often take three steps forward and two steps back in our growth and pursuit to find and live that truth.

Science can only hypothesise based on what it knows to be true and/ or what it can measure. So where does that leave all that it doesn't yet know? The scientific method has only really been around for a few hundred years, but no matter how tight the technique, the scientific method can use in its experiments only information that is already known. So, if we didn't know until a Harvard University study in 1932 that blood can course through the veins of the foetus of a chicken while it's still in its egg *before* its heart has properly developed[15] – and most of the world is still blissfully unaware of that finding nearly eighty-five years later – what more don't we know about life, our bodies, and the purpose and potential of our human heart?

Science continues to evolve and uncover evidence that there's very much more to know about where we come from and how we work. There are many studies going on into the links between the heart and the brain, and how our minds and our bodies can work better together than we currently allow them to or give them credit for. There's a lot being uncovered about our spiritual source and humanity thousands of years ago, and what led to our organised religions, dogmas, and associated fears. There is a lot of growing evidence and change, in the medical world particularly, in relation to placebo effects and how our brain works with our heart and vice versa.

Sometimes it's easy to either feel alone or feel part of a big horrible world we don't like being in – sometimes we feel a bit of both. But the world itself isn't horrible; it's what humanity has done to it that makes it horrible. We live with fear-based everything in a civilisation in which greed tops the hierarchy.

The world itself is actually amazing. It's a miracle, it's magic, it's energy, it's pure beauty, and we're a resourceful, privileged, and connected part of it. We can live well and we can work on our own healing energy to allow our inner lights to love, give, and shine. We can prevent *dis*-ease by focusing on living with *ease*. The world and the universe are there for us, are all around us, and they help us to create in whichever way we choose.

So, accept yourself for what you are, what you have, and what you can do. Accept yourself as you are *now* – a perfect, beautiful human being living in a complex and difficult society, doing the best you can with what you've got. Forgive yourself, forgive others, and change small things to bring that ease into your life. Choose optimism, be creative, and embrace your unique beauty and perfection. Choose love, appreciation, and compassion. Consciously think of yourself as part of something that's far bigger than humanity – and much, *much* nicer. Choose to step over and above the fear-based world we live in and reach out higher towards a universe that supports you, believes in you, and is there – has always been there – to help you if you can fight off some of the thorny overgrowth and pursue your colourful field of dreams.

There are many in the world on the same creative adventure you and I are on. Reach out if you feel alone; I'm here and so are plenty of others. More and more all the time. It's a whole new, amazing direction. Collective consciousness is shifting.

> Know the world in yourself. Never look for yourself in the
> world, for this would be to project your illusion.[16]
> Ancient Egyptian proverb

Doodle, Scribble, Create!

You're human.

Consider something that has been sitting stale inside you that you haven't been able to shift – maybe a past misdemeanour, event, or some words you said to someone.

There are a lot more tips to come throughout the course of the book that will help you to remove some of these blocks, but for the time being, choose one and start to work on it. Take time to really doodle, scribble, create forgiveness and acceptance of yourself so that you can start to detach, move on, and live true to you. Identify anything you need to do, any steps you need to take, to enable that forgiveness and acceptance. Treat yourself with love and compassion. Do you need to contact anyone or take any action to repair any past deeds?

Again, this can be confronting, but if you accept your perfection and your beauty, you'll find yourself starting to have a strength and an inner knowing that you have to step outside your comfort zone and confront what needs to be confronted. And confrontation doesn't have to be an argument or cross words or defensiveness. Grant yourself the strength and power to approach objectively what needs to be dealt with.

You may not be forgiven, and you may not restore past relationships. You may not 'fix' what was 'broken'. However, if you've addressed issues in the best way you can, with love, patience, compassion, care, and humility, you'll know that you have done what you can, and you can properly start to move on from the event. The rest remains with the other party, if there is another party. Responsibility is a two-way street, and if you've done your bit, and you've done it considerately, with generosity, and with love, you can be comfortable with that. Respect the other person and allow them to choose how to deal with your actions.

Similarly, you might just know you need to do something for yourself. There may be no one else involved. Whatever burden or burdens you're carrying around here, think about what you can do to address them. Apply what you've been learning so far, research anything that will help you, and remember that there are plenty more tips you can use that will help you as we progress through the book.

You may like to search for meditations on forgiveness and self-acceptance.

Lesley MacCulloch

You Are Love

While you are a perfect and beautiful human, know that you were also born full of love. Love is *you*, and *you* are love. Where's your mirror? This is everything that you are and can be. Say it: 'I am love, I am loving, I live love, I am loved.' Remember to look yourself in the eye.

'I am perfect the way I am. I am beautiful and I am love. I give love, I receive love, I am surrounded by love. I love, I love, I love.' Think hearts, think of your fourth chakra centre at your chest, the colour green, take deep breaths into your fourth chakra, *Anahata,* and think pure love.

Say it, say it again, and then say it again.

And then remember the Beatles – 'All you need is love. Love is all you need.'

This is what I meant when I wrote earlier about repetition and consistency. Challenge your conditioned life-long beliefs about yourself and feed yourself the truth as often as you can throughout your day. The truth is that you are quite right, right now, the way you are. You're a beautiful human being who's got everything to offer, but first of all you need to offer it to yourself. Your truth will also help to balance your fifth chakra at your throat.

♥ Balance your heart chakra with love.

If you don't feel love or loved, let that be an indication that there's something or things in your life that may need to be changed. Externally, perhaps you're spending time in circles and networks that don't serve you well. As it is with many of our issues or hang-ups, however, the change might need to be within yourself. Perhaps you're closed off to the love that *is* around you and *is* in you. There's every chance that you are totally loved, but because you don't love yourself, you warp or do not even perceive what other people are offering you. Perhaps you fear love, don't trust love, avoid love. Perhaps you ignore love or deny that there *is* love around you and within you.

It's a hard and heavy weight, avoiding love, but think back to Part One and all the emotions and happiness that fall under the aspect of true love. Gratitude, joy, kindness, acceptance, forgiveness, confidence, bliss, happiness, trust, peace, harmony – and that's only touching the surface. Imagine how you could *feel* if you let more of that into your life. Imagine how much lighter and freer you'd feel if you felt love, displayed love, gave love, received love, and lived more love.

In our stress, we carry around a lot of resistance. Resistance is heavy; it weighs us down. If we can give of ourselves and open our hearts, we attract more of those loving, peaceful, 'easy' emotions. We always have our guard up. We are scared that, if we show love, we'll be on the back foot and be 'caught out', that the world will 'get' us in some way for being weak. But this isn't the case. We're stronger living and standing by who we *are* than we are living by our egos and allowing ourselves to be guided by external parties and the fear aspects of life.

Remember: love vibrates at the highest frequency.

We are scared of love. We take the focus off ourselves and put love back on the weed-smoking hippies of the sixties and seventies. We are scared to touch. We are scared to hold hands or arms with someone who isn't our spouse, or our parents or children. We are self-conscious of any form of closeness or proximity to each other. And we most certainly don't talk about love unless it's with those family members – or a poster of some icon who looks good or can sing or act.

Yet we can give and receive so much joy for opening ourselves up to love someone for their amazing and unconditional friendship, for what that person means to us; for the connection we have to them in a certain moment or environment and which doesn't need to last a lifetime. Love is beautiful, and love is wide open. Love is up in the sky and all around you. Love is deep within you; it's your fire to be free.

Let yourself be free. Think, be, and do 'love'. Put fear and your ego back in their place. Challenge your ego. You no longer want your ego as a full-time attendant. Every time your ego feeds you to believe you're not good enough, that you're too fat, clumsy, stupid, hopeless – or leads you to believe you're superior – let love remind it that you're perfect the way you are. We drop things. We can sometimes do with the health benefits of toning up a bit or losing some weight. We can do something in the spur of the moment that we wouldn't normally do, or act like we're better than others. None of this means we *are* that behaviour. You *are* what's inside: a beautiful, perfect being with the power, strength, and will to change everything you want to change. You just need to believe you *can* instead of believing that you can't possibly and that others are better.

You are going to let yourself be free.

💜 Love is life.

Tell your ego that right now. Tell your ego you've appreciated how it has looked out for you all these years, but that things are now going to change. Let it know you're changing your journey and that you're going to be travelling alone now. Tell it you're choosing love, that you're reclaiming your power and no longer want to be living with fear (doubt, anger, worry, guilt, embarrassment, shame, feelings of unworthiness and hopelessness).

Tell your ego you are joy, peace, harmony, graciousness, kindness, honesty, optimism, fun, contentedness, wholesomeness, positivity. Tell it that you are grounded and confident, and that it's no longer going to be in control of you and your self-esteem.

As you view *you*, view love as your companion, your friend, your constant. I often carry a piece of rose quartz in my pocket, and it serves me throughout my day in two ways. Sometimes I inadvertently touch it or feel it there and it reminds me to think, feel, and act with love. It helps me to stay in a place of love, to proceed through my day with love, to put a smile on my face and expect the best. Other times I touch it and ask myself the best way to act, or what decision to make when I have to make a decision, no matter how small. This pause guides me to be able to hear and then make the love-based decision coming to me from inside, and that's right for me, rather than to proceed with fear into a confronting or defensive situation. I sometimes ask my crystal what it would do in a situation. When you listen to that – when you listen to what's inside you – you immediately know the answer. You may not believe in the power of crystals; in fact, you could just as easily put a common rock from your driveway in your pocket. It's what that thing in your pocket signifies that's important: the fact that it reminds you to listen to *you*. Esther and Jerry Hicks have a series of books based on the teachings of a group of non-physical entities known, collectively, as Abraham. Abraham speaks of an 'easy button'. This can be anything you have around your house or in your pocket, as long as it reminds you that things, life, decisions are easy. After a visit to Prague, a colleague of mine gave me a five-crown coin to use as my easy button. For weeks and weeks the two of us carried our easy buttons around, and they certainly gave us laughter when we may have been drawn towards other less productive emotions.

Initially, you will find your head overrules your intuition before you've had a chance to even acknowledge that your intuition has given you any guidance. It takes time, but know and feel that you are love.

This morning, I picked up my little book *When I Loved Myself Enough* by Kim McMillen with Alison McMillen. I opened to the page that said, 'When I loved myself enough – forgiving others became irrelevant.'[17]

When you get there you'll know exactly what that means. And you're on the way, superstar!

Doodle, Scribble, Create!

Doodle, scribble, create one thing you are going to do to remind yourself throughout your day that there's another way to react and that it's a way based in love.

You Are You

That's what – and who – you are. You are *you*. You are your light. You are your truth. You are everything you've wanted to do, say, and emit but haven't just in case someone might 'think' one way or another of you.

If that's too difficult a concept to grasp, here, then, is what you're *not*:

- You're not your job.
- You're not your age.
- You're not your role in life.
- You're not your dress or trouser size.
- You're not your income.
- You're not your mortgage.
- You're not your house, your flat, your lodging, your sofa.
- You're not what your school, your society, your head have been telling you that you are your whole life.
- You're not your phone, your computer, the *things* that you have or think you need in life.

Yet you allow yourself to be defined by those things, to feel condemned by others for not having or being something different. Some of these things are material things. *None* of these things is important. None of them is *you*.

When you allow that *you* to breathe, you will realise – and accept – that none of the things in the list above makes any difference to your bigger picture, to your energy life, or to your inner being. It's only other people and your comparisons with other people that make you think they do. Free yourself up from these confines! Let your heart sing. Reach high! Your heart and soul are *you*. And you *are* energy and life. *You* are the deepest part of you; *you* are your core.

You are your spirit, your soul, your energy, your vibrations, your feelings, your emotions, your heart, your light. Remember back to Part One – you are pure energy, and you are part of the energy around you.

♥ Free yourself and spread your wings.

I went away on a vision quest one summer. In the ten days I was away, not one of the eight people I was with asked me, 'What do you do?' Can you imagine how refreshing it is to be in the company of people who do not define you by what you do in your life? That just wasn't important to them.

Neither did we know or need to know each other's ages. We were one. We were connected by our love of our natural surroundings, our respect for and unconditional acceptance of each other and what we brought to the group, our reasons for being there, and our appreciation of time alone in and with the elements.

'So what did you talk about?' some asked me afterwards. They were puzzled and curious, not quite able to believe such information wouldn't be part of a single conversation, never mind numerous conversations over ten days. We talked about who we were, and we listened to each other. We shared our experiences, and we were acknowledged, we were accepted, we were given space to talk uninterrupted about things we wanted to talk about. And sometimes we didn't talk very much at all.

We were respected for who we were and what we chose to give, and we delighted in speaking peacefully, one at a time, with space to think, and where silence wasn't awkward or avoided – indeed it was relished, inhaled, and absorbed. We were granted the space to share, to 'think aloud', to laugh, cry, and just be in the fold of people who were comfortable with and in silence, who accepted and who listened, reflected, and acknowledged.

Not one single person knew or needed to know anything about how old I was or what I did for a living – not that discussions about age and career were barred; a few did talk about their occupations if the topic was relevant to their discussion. But mostly we shared far more depth and love than either of those two topics induce.

What a glorious opportunity to *re*-realise what's important and how much time we spend in our communities, societies, and environments talking about superficial things, things that don't matter or that aren't 'us' and that don't represent the person we are or the light we shine.

♥ Speak peacefully and from within.

It's only just recently, too, that I've really become aware of how good we all are – indeed what experts we are – at not saying what we think. And I don't mean saying what we think to offend; I mean saying what we think in a considered, courteous, loving way that speaks of who we are, at the same time allowing others room for their perspectives, opinions, and views.

But we don't say what we think, not even in a loving, objective, compassionate way because we don't want to upset people. We've forgotten that we can say things that don't necessarily 'agree' with others in such a way as to not be confronting or aggressive. We can disagree without the lack of agreement causing an argument or a falling-out. Just because we say something potentially adverse doesn't mean we're going to rock the boat; it just means we should be considerate and gentle in the way we say it.

Neither do we allow others the capacity, respect, strength, maturity, and wisdom to choose to accept what we say in the way we intend it to be received. Instead we expect their judgement and some other fear response, and so, in effect, we too are judging.

Years back, when I worked in the corporate world, leader colleagues of mine would upset their staff by bringing up at performance appraisals minor issues that should have been dealt with when they arose. If we all started communicating and chatting about issues when they arise, when they are small, incidental, and easy to discuss, we could avoid unnecessary confrontations that develop when eventually they are addressed. Staff members didn't know they'd done anything 'wrong' until four, five, six months later when their leader decided to confront them with something that should have been discussed and dealt with months earlier outside the confines of a formal appraisal meeting as part of everyday normal constructive communication.

Think also about potentially adverse or confrontational situations with neighbours: You want them to trim their raggedy hedges, you want them to stop parking over your driveway, you want them to put their bin somewhere else. These are just examples. The thing is, do you moan and complain about what they're doing or not doing, expecting them to be able to read your mind, reluctant to approach them as it'll be too confronting? Or do you go up to their door with a smile to explain *nicely* that you're having trouble parking because their car is in a bit of an awkward spot. Reverse the situation. If someone came to your door with a smile and a nice tone of voice and a bit of chit chat, you'd be far more likely to listen to what they had to say – and *why* they were saying it – than you would if the same person arrived with what seemed to be conflict and argument in mind. If you can't manage what they're asking, at least you're having a conversation and you may be able to offer an alternative plan, or some friendly understanding and negotiation.

💙 Speak of who *you* are – allow your heart do the talking.

What's happening in these situations is that we're all looking *outside*. We're worried about approaching others in case their reaction isn't accepting. We jump to conclusions. Yet the longer we leave things, the bigger they become for our ego, and the more difficult they become to address. We turn the molehill into a mountain, and we end up carrying a plethora of fear-related emotions around in relation to what should have been one simple conversation. By the time we have the conversation not only have we built it up in our head to be a major confrontation, we have almost definitely created and attracted the outcome we have been expecting.

If we believe enough in what we want or need to say – and keep it in perspective! – then we are more able to speak from our hearts and listen to and accept the responses of others for what they are. We will be able to have conversations instead of conflicts, arguments and fallings-out.

Don't let your ego tell you that everything's got to become a fight. Let your heart tell you that you can communicate openly, honestly, objectively, and with a smile. People are much more likely to work with you if that's your approach too.

♥ Live gently.

Are You Your Values? Are Your Values You?

Do you know what your values are? Are you aware of your values? Do you allow your values to guide you through your life? You do have values, but you may never have stopped and consciously considered what they are.

Some may disagree, but in my view, your true values are usually representative of *you*. They're maybe the first most tangible sign of the real you that's shining your light inside. And often, just as we do to our shining lights, we bury our values deep inside and ignore them when it's easier to pretend we either believe otherwise, or have no strong feelings one way or the other.

When you're asked to behave in a manner that doesn't sit well with you, the reason it doesn't sit well with you is usually that it conflicts with your values.

That's *you* talking to you. At those moments do you convince, push, or make yourself act in the way you're being asked to and ignore the messages coming from inside? Or do you listen to the messages coming to you from deep down inside about whether this is the right direction or decision for you at this point in time. Remember, bad feelings are indicators. They're messages that something's not quite as it should be. All you have to do then is consider what's not quite right and make changes accordingly.

Your values comprise what is important to *you* and *only* you. When you are quite clear on what they are, they help you to live true to *you* and they help you to retain your integrity, your morals, and your ethics. We're not interested in anybody else. Your values represent *you*. What do *you* love doing, who do *you* love being, what's important to *you*?

Your values are based on your deep beliefs and on your outlook to life. Your values are aspects and views you have of life that are deeply meaningful and important to *you*. Your values represent what's true and honest about life to you; they're your views. Think about your true character, your personality, your traits, your beliefs, your feelings. Consider what actually matters to you. What do you feel strongly about? Often in our lives, we can be put upon or easily led by others, by dishonesty, by things we don't believe in, by people we don't believe in. It can be momentarily easier to ignore our values and our truth if to live by them makes us feel embarrassed, self-conscious, threatened, or at risk; however, often the consequences of ignoring our values come back to bite us in other deeper, more serious ways. These ways can be more difficult to amend. To be true to yourself, sticking with your values and finding a way to step over or work through the embarrassment, the self-consciousness, or the threat is the better, easier, smarter way to go over the longer term.

Delayed gratification, one of M. Scott Peck, MD's four basic tools of discipline in his book, *The Road Less Travelled*, is better in the long run than the self-serving, impulsive whim of the immediate reward.

Values can be based around all sorts of experiences and emotions and attributes:

- They might be based around security, your children, your family, feeling safe, feeling comfortable, feeling secure.
- You might need to get outside and run for half an hour a day.
- It might be bungee-jumping you need, and getting your adrenalin rush.
- It might simply be being honest, trustworthy, and true to yourself.
- Integrity is a value; fairness, courage, peace, silence, being at one with nature could all be values.
- Your values might include being reliable, being appreciative, being thorough, being on time.
- You might make sure that you laugh every day; you might not be at your best until you have danced, or sung, or shaken or stretched your body.

♥ Get to know your values; get to know *you*.

Your values could include being kind, thoughtful, compassionate, empathetic. You might have a strong, deep need to help others, grow your own crops, learn something new every day. If you're here today working through this book then it's likely that feeling happy, content, joyful, feeling more pleasure in your life, growing inside your heart and soul are important to you.

I have quite a number of values; I'll give you some examples. It's important for me, in a work situation, to feel challenge, fulfilment, and satisfaction. In my life in general, I need to live honestly; I need to be trusted, dependable, and reliable; and I need to feel I'm helping other people to believe in themselves. I am deeply appreciative of things and opportunities that come my way, and I need to do what I tell others I will do. I absolutely need to be in nature and the outdoors at some point every day. I need colour, flowers, soil, grass, trees, and sky. And I need silence and time alone regularly. These few values are important values for me, and if I don't live true to them I feel empty, lost, frustrated, or a bit sick inside.

The exercise that follows in the next Doodle, Scribble, Create! box will help you to identify your values. Don't make it harder than it needs to be. Your values are simply your truth – what's important to you and what helps, or will help, you thrive. Even if you think you know what your values are, take time to work through the exercise because you change as you evolve through life, and you might be surprised at what comes up.

If you spend time doing things you don't enjoy, being places or with people you don't enjoy, *don't write these things down!* Similarly, if there are things you've done all your life, if there is a character trait you have been all your life but you don't believe it portrays *you*, then don't write it down. If you spot any inconsistencies, conflicts, or opposites as you're creating, have a look at them and consider the truth in them. Which one is stronger? Which one is really your value? Just because something is a regular in your life doesn't mean it's right or important or the real, live, shining you. Your values are your *truth*.

The following creation will help to remind you of what's important to you and who you really are. Get to know yourself again.

♥ Your values are your truth.

Doodle, Scribble, Create!

Your values.

Doodle, scribble, create your truth — the values that represent the true, deep-down, shining you. Take your time; there's no hurry. You may find you want to come back to this a few times as you realise your deep truth.

Doodle, Scribble, Create!

Now forge a plan for the coming days, weeks, and months to ensure you live your values. These are your truths. They are you. They matter to you, and you're no longer going to pretend otherwise.

Doodle, scribble, create at least three ways you will deliver, display, and live true to your self, your inner light, and your values.

You Are the Light

To SUMMARISE EVERYTHING THAT YOU ARE, stand in front of the mirror and smile. Look yourself in the eye and keep smiling. Now tell yourself you are perfect the way you are.

Tell yourself you are beautiful. Tell yourself that you accept yourself as a human, with all your human traits, and that you forgive yourself for past misdemeanours and things you'd like to change but can't. Tell yourself that you're moving onwards and upwards to live true to your inner light and that twinkle in your eye.

Smile, look yourself in the eye, and tell yourself that you love who you are and what you are. Using your name, tell yourself you love *you* just the way you are.

Stretch your arms to the sky, keep looking yourself in the eye, and tell yourself you're on your way to living true to *you*. Prepare yourself to be open to the love that is all around you, and tell yourself you are going to feel more love-based emotions than fear-based emotions in your life from now on.

And finally tell yourself your values. As if you would to a friend, talk to yourself about how you feel to have properly identified or confirmed your true values. Tell yourself you are now going to live true to yourself and to your values and that you'd love some help along the way from your heart, your inner wisdom, and your little light inside.

Do this over and over, each and every day, as often as you can consciously fit it in. Even if you are not in a place where you can look in the mirror, tell it to yourself over and over. If you're doing it in the mirror but don't always want to do it aloud, that's fine! Do it quietly, or lip-sync or mime. However you do it, just do it.

And when your ego butts in, just tell it straight. You will be listening to it on *your* terms. You don't need so many emotional hurdles put in your way. Tell your ego farewell. Have you ever heard the saying 'your ego is not your amigo'? It's time to see it off, send it packing. It no longer protects you in the way it was meant to; it holds you up.

In his Facebook post dated 12 February 2016, American actor, comedian, and motivational speaker, Kyle Cease put it perfectly when he said that our ego is aghast when we allow our love to flow freely 'because it's death to the story of the limited past that we think we are'.[18]

♥ Honour your *now*.

You Can ...

REACH UP TO THE SKY. REACH high. Pretend you're a tree. Go on. Nobody's watching, and even if they were, it's time for us all to *stop caring*.

Reach up. Stretch out. Close your eyes. Smile. Find and feel joy about something. In fact, find and feel the joy in simply doing that.

Say out loud, 'I can, I *can*, I CAN!' Say it loud. Shout it! You don't need me to prompt you. From now on, fit this exercise into your day. This is how I opened this book, on the very first page of the introduction. Do it in front of the mirror. Do it outside. Tell it to the sun! Shout it to the world.

This is where you stop doubting and start believing. This is where you open up to *you* and move away from closed off and stubborn. This is where you *do* instead of *don't*, this is where you *yes* instead of *no*, this is where you embrace with open arms instead of hiding away, avoiding and denying.

This is where you say, 'Yes, *yes*, YES! Let me at it, let me do it, let me see it, let me try it!'

This is where you tell yourself you *can*. You've done a lot of work already, mainly on your beliefs about your world and your beliefs about yourself. This section is also about your beliefs: your beliefs about your confidence and ability. We'll look at some of the more tangible aspects of your life and take steps both to change your behaviours and help you to encourage and allow yourself to believe, embrace, rejoice, and *know* you can. It's your ego head that's doubting you and holding you up; *you*, inside, *can*. And your light's just waiting to shine brighter than it's ever shone for you, on you, and inside you.

Your 'I can' is more important than your IQ!

> When I was travelling through Calcutta, I met a schoolteacher named Malika Chand. She loved teaching and treated her students as she would her own children, nurturing their potential with great kindness. Her perennial motto was 'Your I can is more important than your I.Q.' She was known throughout her community as a person who lived to give, who selflessly served anyone in need.[19]
> Robin Sharma

You *can* do everything this section is going to suggest, and you can do more if you want to. You can take action, you can carry out your own research, reading, and investigation. You can explore new information and experiences. You can make different choices, you can review your beliefs, you can make decisions that might surprise yourself, never mind others. Yes, others might look at you as if you've grown horns since the last time they saw you because that type of behaviour or decision is not what they expect of you, or what you're 'supposed' to say or do – that's not the you they know. And, yes, others might talk about you behind your back, but you can also deal with that and you can choose to remember that judging you is their choice and issue, not anything to do with what you're getting on with in your life being *you*.

You can't ever do anything about others making judgements of you. Whatever you are, whoever you are, others will judge. They will be doing that already anyway, so at least if you're changing, you're giving them something worthwhile to ponder about. They might actually want to know what it is you're doing! It's time to move on from the judgements of society and friends and family members. You neither require their judgement, nor care about their judgement. Just let them be and let *you* free.

You really can have a happier life. You really can expose yourself to confidence and belief and a brighter, shinier, calmer way of living. You really can have less struggle, less defeat, less gloom in your life. You really can emerge like a butterfly from your cocoon of old and fly high, my earth friend.

And you can have all of that, not by the activities you enjoy or the people you see – although of course these things make you happy and less gloomy – but by looking inside and changing your belief systems. Of course your hobbies and your friends and your family members bring you joy, but they're external sources, and they're not always there to bring you joy. And you can't put the responsibility for your own happiness onto others; otherwise, you pass the buck and blame them when you're unhappy. You're not responsible for anyone else's happiness, so how can they be responsible for yours? We can't change each other; we find what we need inside, not outside.

No, we're not told that at school or in life, but that's the way of it.

We find what we need inside.

You now need to take responsibility for your joy. Only you can help yourself to be in a happier state more of the time. You are your friend and supporter, your encouragement and your personal guide. Remember, you're the one who has the power, not other people or things. You have inside you what it takes to make your life more enjoyable, and you are responsible for enabling that enjoyment; it is not the responsibility of other people. You can't rely on external sources for your happiness, ease and well-being. Listen to your intuition – your *self* – for guidance through your days and your life, and constructively consider the messages from your ego.

❤ Reframe your life – become the star.

The big step is getting to that point where your intuition, your instinct, your inner being comes first and that you hear it, listen to it, recognise it – and start to heed it – over and above the messages coming from your head.

I want to help you get to a stage where you are happy, content, and not bored when you have time to do nothing at all. I want you to realise the beauty, the enrichment, and the power in doing nothing. Everything in our lives makes us feel as if we should be *doing* all of the time. If we're not doing, we're viewed as boring, lazy, worthless, or useless, and because we expect that condemnation from our external world, we feed that message to ourselves. But why? Where did that message come from, and why can't we enjoy just being in the present? We spend a *lot* of time doing things that aren't important and that don't matter, so why not spend more time simply enjoying our space, our peace, and our world for what it is?

The message, as usual, comes from our surroundings, from our external lives, and from our heads. (Remember it's our heads that listen to what others say we should be being or doing.) And we allow those external sources to be 'right', to dictate what our lives should or shouldn't be, what our time should or shouldn't be spent doing. It seems to matter more to have all the toys put away and dust-free skirting boards in case of visitors than it does to spend time with ourselves or those we love. We allow our minds to make us feel we should always be doing something. Even if we're sitting down enjoying five or ten minutes time out, we can hardly allow ourselves to relax without putting upon ourselves that we should be elsewhere, doing. We seem to always be itching to get moving again. We keep seeing and thinking of things that 'need' to be done around us. Either we don't allow ourselves to relax, or we beat ourselves up for doing so, or even for just trying to enjoy our lives or to be with ourselves for one single moment.

We often think ourselves into feeling that we *should* be *doing* something all the time. But the simple fact is that we shouldn't, needn't, and don't have to be *doing*.

You *can* think, feel and do differently. And you *can* do *nothing*.

♥ Think 'be' instead of 'do' sometimes.

You Can Open Up

Opening up means behaving differently. You question things. You challenge your thinking. You react differently and consider more broadly much of what's going on in and around your life. Opening up means inviting change, such as new information and different possibilities. Opening up means welcoming. You seize, you embrace. You try different things; you listen to different information, music, and points of view; you meet different people. Opening up expands your horizons, deepens your wisdom, and broadens your mind.

And if you keep reaching up to the sky as often as you can, you will open up from your heart (not to mention how great that stretch is for your body).

I mentioned M. Scott Peck, MD, back when we were talking about values, and I'd like to use some of his words here to demonstrate how being open is one of our inherent truths and a discipline that we've denied ourselves for most of our lives. In his book, *The Road Less Travelled*, Dr Peck talks about humans having four discipline tools: delay of gratification, acceptance of responsibility, dedication to truth, and balancing.

In his chapter entitled 'Dedication to Reality'[20] he points out that 'truth is reality' and that 'the more clearly we see the reality of the world, the better equipped we are to deal with the world.'

The less clearly we see the reality of the world – the more our minds are befuddled by falsehood, misperceptions and illusions – the less able we will be to determine correct courses of action and make wise decisions. Our view of reality is like a map with which to negotiate the terrain of life. If the map is true and accurate, we will generally know where we are, and if we have decided where we want to go, we will generally know how to get there. If the map is false and inaccurate, we generally will be lost.

Hence, if we're not open, we don't see the truth. We don't even allow ourselves the opportunity to see the truth. If we spend our lives listening to others, being told what to believe, and watching the news and other mainstream media, we are ignoring our capacity and our choice to inform ourselves about what actually *is* going on in the world. We grow up believing that our maps are complete, and that the information we have is correct and all that we need. Because of this, we tend to ignore new information about the world in which we live.

Dr Peck goes on to say:

> While this is obvious, it is something that most people to a greater or lesser degree choose to ignore. They ignore it because our route to reality is not easy. First of all, we are not born with maps, we have to make them, and the making requires effort. The more effort we make to appreciate and perceive reality, the larger and more accurate our maps will be. But many do not want to make this effort. Some stop making it by the end of adolescence. Their maps are small and sketchy, their views of the world narrow and misleading. By the end of middle age most people have given up the effort. They feel certain that their maps are complete

and their *Weltanschauung* [philosophy; view of live] is correct (indeed, even sacrosanct), as if they are tired. Only a relative and fortunate few continue until the moment of death exploring the mystery of reality, ever enlarging and refining and redefining their understanding of the world and what is true.

But the biggest problem of map-making is not that we have to start from scratch, but that if our maps are to be accurate we have to continually revise them. The world itself is constantly changing.

These paragraphs speak volumes on their own and need no further explanation. Nothing is set in stone; everything in our world, even science – *particularly* science and particularly quantum physics in the last ten to twenty years – is ever evolving. And if we don't open up to the news, progress, and reality of our world that *isn't* being delivered via mainstream media, we will continue progressing through life being guided by our small, sketchy, inaccurate, and often completely false maps.

Scary.

So, open up. That's it. That's the message: open up – and know that you *can*. Opening up could set you free. Allow yourself the opportunity even just to consider that something other than what you do, believe, or think might be possible. And then take advantage of it!

♥ Challenge your mind and open your world.

But where do you start? How do you go from a lifetime of being closed, to opening your heart, head and mind to 'new', to 'different', to 'variety'? We'll talk through a few different strategies shortly, but to get a sense of the subtleties of what we're doing here, here are a few points to challenge your thinking and encourage open-mindedness:

- **We are all the same.** When you really feel, believe, and embrace the vastness of what's up there and out there, beyond the ends of your fingertips, as you're reaching high and shouting that you can, you'll appreciate that vastness, your smallness, and the real true fact that you actually *can*. Of course you can. Why wouldn't you be able to? If you're such a small part of this vastness, then so is everybody else, so what makes all these judges and supposed figures of superiority or authority around you any better than you? We're all just picking our way through life here on earth. We are all a part of the enormity of what really *is*, doing the best we can with what we've been given and what we've allowed ourselves to be, do, and have. Others will know things that you don't, but you know things that they don't. Others might have a professional role in which they are entitled to act as your superior, but that is only a role; it is not *them*. They were not born superior or better than you, however much they act as if they were, or you allow yourself to feel that they were. Your general practitioner (GP) is a person who went to university to learn about helping people to get better. Just because you chose not to follow that route doesn't make your GP better than you. The police are people at work, doing a job they're paid to do, in a uniform they're told to wear. Your teachers are only as good as their own learning, experiences, openness, and ability to facilitate information. You're in the process of opening your mind to the universe of possibility that you're a part of, and many of the individuals in these roles not only haven't done that, but would discourage you from doing so. Know that you are not less than they are. Know that they are not better than you. We are all the same.
- **You are already open.** You've managed to get to this stage in the book. Already you've proven you can challenge yourself to consider new or different information, new or different knowledge, developments and creations. Indeed, you're creating your own new world yourself through

your doodling, scribbling, and creating. You've shown that you're open to changes, to opportunities, and to taking back responsibility and power. This is you being open. You're trying new things in new ways, and seeing different points of view. You're opening up and filling yourself with love. You're opening up to *feeling* – feeling hope, feeling the depth and power of true awe, feeling humble, and feeling present.

- **Opinions of others are insignificant.** As you reach high and feel deeply that you *can*, you'll also realise in that vastness how insignificant other people's opinions are, and how lacking in any sense it is that we spend most of our lives worrying about what other people might think. This is your life, and it's time you started living it.

- **Pay attention and feel free.** Pay attention to the feelings you have when you open up physically and mentally. At first you'll notice these feelings only briefly, but with time and patience, you'll get better at noticing how free you feel, how a weight has been removed when you realise there's quite a different and viable way of looking at and thinking about the things you've always denied, discounted, disputed, ignored, renounced, rejected, and avoided.

- **Risk the embarrassment; what's the worst that could happen?** What's a bit of momentary discomfort? Why avoid something your whole life because of a few minutes risk of feeling awkward. Does that sound very rational? Look at the size of your life, and look at the little step involved in doing that one small thing. If you don't do things you want to do because people might talk, or you might fall, or you might 'fail', or you might say something silly, or you might feel confronted, or you might not get the job, or – possibly worse – you might get the job, then what! Then you will never, ever feel wholly satisfied or fulfilled. (I should mention that, in my view, there's no such thing as failing. You might 'fail' to achieve the specific thing you set out to do in the first place, but you will have grown in so many other ways by the simple fact that you've tried that you can't possibly have failed.) If you do not try, you will always wonder and you will harbour fear-related emotions including resentment and grudges. Open up your mind, your heart, your soul, and go do these things – all of them. Do everything and anything that you'd love to do but that you've decided will make you feel awkward or embarrassed or scared. You will open up, you will inflate, and you will grow from every single one of these experiences. Any awkwardness or embarrassment or fear will be superseded by elation, joy, and the knowledge and acceptance that you *can*. You might even be surprised to find you succeed without any awkwardness, embarrassment or fear after all!

• **Empowerment is energising.** Notice that, once you open up, you learn, you become informed, you think differently, you realise things. You may become less opinionated because you realise there are so many ways to think about one thing. You might find you bite your tongue and listen more, taking more in. Becoming informed allows you to take ownership of and responsibility for yourself and your beliefs, and taking ownership and being responsible is incredibly empowering. Be open to the amazing light feeling of empowerment. Again, this is your life, make now your time to live it.

• **Ask for or seek support.** If you're nervous, or it all feels just too much for you and you're becoming overwhelmed, there are people like me around you. Ease away from people who are helping to keep you closed down and feeling small; rather, approach people who will encourage you to open up as wide as you can, who will help you to reach up high, to fly, to open up and shine. They're out there, and you don't have to look very hard to find them. Look for holistic groups and fairs, meditation groups, spiritual communities. Check through your library or your local community or yoga centre for what's available in your area. Look for 'meet up' groups that feel right for you. You *can* change the circles you're in, the activities in which you participate, the friends you have. You *can* open up and reach out to people who will accept you the perfect way you are, embrace the beauty in you, encourage the human that is you, and who will empower you to be, feel, and display love in ways you've never experienced before.

Let's do an exercise before we move on to some of the more specific ways in which you can open up.

Doodle, Scribble, Create!

Doodle, scribble, create that you can! Include in your creation what opening up means to you and how you are going about opening up more and more to life and what's around you.

You Can Accept

When you open up, you begin to realise and accept that there's more out there in our world and in the universe, that there's more to everything than meets the eye. There's more to someone's behaviour than is perhaps evident initially. There's more behind the news than we're actually being told. There's more to the world than just what we've chosen to believe up till now. There's a lot more to us – our bodies, how we work – than we've ever been taught.

The more you read, learn, and research; the further you stretch; the deeper you investigate; the more you realise there's a lot going on within the folds and confines of your daily life and your world that you simply don't know about. And the more you realise that, the easier it can be to accept that things are ever changing and evolving.

At the same time, however, the more you learn and realise about yourself and your connection to the universe and its elements, the harder it can be to accept things for what they are. Whatever is inside *you,* you can change and affect. Whatever is outside you, you mostly can't. I could go round in philosophical circles, but accepting is really about choosing to accept the external components of your world that you can't change, or taking constructive steps to try do something about them if you're allowing them to adversely affect your life.

Accepting that something 'is' the way it is, or that someone 'is' the way they are can be difficult to do when you have your own judgements and perceptions about people and life. It can be challenging to accept a system of bureaucracy, a curriculum of learning, or process of officialdom.

The more you can either accept or manage the external features of your life that you can't change, the more able you will be to keep yourself open, clear, and free of negative energy. Remember your chakras, your energy centres. You want them as balanced as possible.

Anger, judgement, and perceptions that bog you down just mess everything up inside and lead to stress and fear-based behaviours. Live from your heart and accept.

Accept by Releasing, Detaching, and Letting Go

When I talk about accepting, I don't mean sitting back and passively accepting every single thing in your life as being something you can't change.

What I do mean is allowing yourself to release things that annoy you or make you angry; allowing yourself to detach from people and things that upset you or agitate you or stress you. In Part One I discussed your free will to make choices. I discussed your energy and how the law of attraction works for you and with you – so the more you allow yourself to get upset or angry about things, the more you'll attract things that make you upset and angry. By choosing to acknowledge and accept that the traits of certain people annoy you, you'll be able to rise above the negative energy that corresponds with the annoyance you feel. Accepting what *is* enables you to use your precious energy more wisely. There are probably things about you that annoy them. Accept that we're all different. Rather than focusing on who or what's annoying you, seek inside yourself for ways to deal with the situation.

Here are some ways you might deal with an annoying situation:

- Consciously focus inside, or on something you find acceptable. Do not give a negative situation your attention.
- Choose to say only nice or neutral things.
- Remember that other people's opinions and attitudes tell a story about them. They're not directed at you; neither are they personal.
- Smile and take a deep breath.
- Pause – or smile and take a deep breath – before you speak. This helps to allow a heated moment to pass, keeping a

conflict in perspective. As you're taking your breath, focus on its journey into your being and not on how much the situation is annoying you.

- Sit or stand inwardly still and take a few deep breaths – in through your nose, out through your mouth – filling yourself up with clean air and oxygen. Then get on with whatever it was you were doing.
- Move away from the situation if that is possible.
- Consider whether or not you're overreacting. Listen inside for the answer. Your ego will always say you're not – but what are *you* saying?

♥ Choose to say nice things and come from a loving place.

What if You Can't Accept

If there are things you think you can change, or want to change, then choose to take those things on in a concerted, focused manner, loaded up with the right feelings about them and without making them personal vendettas through which you can simply release your own agitation.

If you want to front a crusade about a system of bureaucracy, or a curriculum of learning, or a process of officialdom, then you have the free will to do so. Choose that path and take objective non-emotive steps towards making your point for change, and do it assertively, decisively, and with your heart as well as your head. Do take appropriate steps and listen attentively to what's going on inside. Aung San Suu Kyi didn't do what she did for Burma by lying back and accepting. Mother Teresa, Mahatma Gandhi, Nelson Mandela, Rosa Parks ... where does the list end? None of these people did what they did by passively accepting. But they did what they did by following their hearts and taking action with love, compassion, gentleness, and care. They did what they did by standing strong, living their truths, shining their lights, using their own free will, and listening to their hearts rather than being bitter, angry, aggressive, or any other fear-related emotion.

> ♥ Stand strong, live your truth, shine your light,
> use your free will, act with love.

I was recently at a funeral of a friend of a friend who had lived a free-spirit lifestyle doing or not doing things as he chose. While this man was fun loving and peaceful, he had very strong feelings about certain things, including the role – indeed the necessity – of the government. He struggled to accept the existence of the government in his country and in his life. But while he couldn't 'accept', he did not spend time being bitter and miserable about something he couldn't change. Instead, he chose to take decisive, constructive action. He started a petition to liquidate the government! His negative feelings and energy would have been turned into a positive as he focussed on doing something about the source of his discontent. As the funeral celebrant said, how many of us wish that we had the courage and the will to provoke such action – yet we *do*. Peter's efforts failed to remove the government; but, as I said earlier, no decisive activity can ever be classed as a failure. The success is in taking the action at all.

In terms of other people, it's none of our business what they think, how they look, how they work, or how they judge us. Isn't that a liberating realisation? It's none of our business how good, bad, or otherwise they are, in our view, at their jobs, being parents, or living their lives. We are here to be open, to live, to love, and to accept. We are not here to get stuck on what other people are doing, thinking, or creating. Yes, of course those other people affect us through their actions, thoughts, and creations, but we then need to look inside at how we wish to deal with that. Doing anything else leads us down a path of misery, resentment, frustration, and dismay. Moving onwards, upwards, and away towards release and detachment leads us up a path of responsibility, accountability, empowerment, and leadership. We beat ourselves up and we drag ourselves down; we make ourselves miserable about things that we cannot do anything about. Yes, of course you have an incompetent or lazy or 'whatever' workmate or committee member who just doesn't get it. Everybody does. But unless you're in a position that enables you to actually do something about the demonstrated behaviours of that person in their role, you can't do anything about it. So what's the point wasting your energy getting miserable or upset about it?

I did a little bit of research into psychopathic behaviour quite a number of years ago. I recall a criminal profiler, Dr John Clarke, had noticed that many of the traits of a criminal psychopath resembled traits of normal, non-criminal, everyday people. He extended his research into the broader community and found that the traits of a criminal psychopath weren't special only to the criminal. He found psychopaths in every walk of life because he determined that the main difference between a psychopath and a 'normal person' was empathy. He found that psychopaths lacked empathy.

> Empathy really is the ability to feel what another person is feeling.
> It's very very important in terms of survival of the human species
> because if nobody really cared or understood what other people
> were feeling it would just cause breakdown of society.[21]
> Dr John Clarke

The Australian Broadcasting Corporation's *Catalyst* programme ran a story on 'Corporate Psychopaths' with Dr Clarke back in 2005.[22] They discussed workplace psychopaths – often managers in large, corporate organisations and conglomerates – and made the point that nobody can or will do anything about these types of people. Nobody is game to challenge them as they strive forward in their careers, ticking recruitment boxes like 'will do what it takes to meet targets'. Corporate psychopaths are manipulative and callous, and often pathological liars, and will find a way to achieve what they want to achieve, potentially at the cost of those around them. Dr Clarke closes the story with, "I want people to be aware that they're not going crazy. It's the workplace psychopath that's the problem, not them."

This is a prime example of how you cannot – and will never – change somebody. It's very much easier on you to accept the situation, the character, the personality, and do what you need to do to deal with it and move on.

I know, I hear you – that's not fair. Life's not fair. But from reading this book you now know it's what you make of life that matters. You're not a victim. Take this information and feel empowered!

Accepting is something to work on rather than read about. We were brought up to judge, so don't expect that you're going to be able to accept everything and everybody overnight. First of all, just identify a few steps to take or behaviours to adopt that will help you accept others into your own life. One of our biggest steps can be accepting ourselves. It could be useful to take this time to keep consciously working on something you've chosen from the section entitled 'You *Are*' and also choose something you're going to do to accept another person, or a situation or thing. Accepting can even be about something we've committed to do and no longer want to do but we feel tied because we gave our word. A lot of people say 'get over it'. This simply means 'accept'.

Here's a handful of examples to help you get your head around really getting better at accepting things instead of making mountains out of molehills and, in the process, making yourself miserable.

❤ Accept *you*, and everything else will be fine.

Accept 1: You choose to hang the washing out. You leave to go to work. It rains before you've even arrived. Rather than cursing all day about the fact that you hung your washing out and it rained, don't say a word. Acknowledge it's rained, and then get over it. You chose to hang the washing out. You knew it could rain.

Accept 2: You're off to work. You hate your job. You've hated it for months. On the way you'll tell as many people as you can that you hate it, and when you arrive you'll remind everybody you work with how much you hate it. This is a deep one because you've been saying this for so long it's a habit. But for starters, stop acknowledging to yourself how much you hate it. Accept that and put your energy into making a list of things you're going to do about it. Then put more of your energy into doing those things. Not only are you making yourself miserable as you live these negative statements and feed yourself a constant flow of doom and gloom, you're ensuring the whole body of people around you, the people who have to come in contact with you in some way throughout the day, are feeling the same. Stop it! It may not be fair that nothing's done about psychopaths, but it's also not fair that others have to listen to and sit around your negativity every day. And, yes, they can do something about that, and maybe they're in the process of doing so. But you can do something too, and you ought to. Do it for everybody's sake, but first and foremost for your own health and well-being.

Accept 3: You just got home from the supermarket only to realise you forgot the most important item you went there for. Accept that you forgot. Either go back out and get it right away, or choose to forget about it and write it down so you won't forget it tomorrow. Don't growl and grizzle about it all night. Don't keep telling yourself and everybody around you that you're an idiot, because you're not. You forgot something at the shops. So be it. Life goes on. Leave it.

Accept 4: The girl at your club really annoys you, and she spoils your night. What exactly is it about the girl that annoys you? What does she do or say? What would happen if you approached the night differently, accepting that you know she's going to be there and expecting that she's *not* going to annoy you? Decide that you're not going to take what she does or says the way you usually do. In fact, have you ever actually spoken to her properly? Have you ever asked her anything about herself, or had a proper conversation with her? Why not decide to try that? Pretend it's the first time you're meeting her and go in open and ready to accept. Could it be that one small thing she did or does has grown into Mount Everest for you, and it's you – your head – that's making more of it than it is and ever was? If none of this works, then go right back to why she annoys you and find the answer and establish how you're going to deal with it inside *you*. Listen to what your inner guidance is telling you to do.

Accept 5: I was feeling quite judged about something recently, and when I stopped and thought about it, I realised that the smaller part of the judgement was coming from external sources; the bulk of the judgement was actually nonexistent and was coming from my own head. I had to step out of that place of judgement and spend a bit of time working out where the judgement was coming from and if it was actually real. Journaling is good for finding answers like this. This just means writing and writing, letting your pen flow without thought, judgement or consideration, as no one will be reading it. Often you can see patterns that explain exactly what's going on. That's when I realised I'd conditioned myself to feel a lot of this judgement based on actions and behaviours I'd been observing for a period of time. Being able to see that helped me to see the whole situation more clearly and to step back into a place of openness and acceptance.

So, there are some everyday examples of how we really can accept more. I was getting a bit tetchy recently about a favour we were doing for a friend. I was getting into a bit of a niggly place about it and had to remember we had offered and agreed to help out. Acceptance helps you to see things with different eyes, and fosters a different and far more open viewpoint. Acceptance really helps us to keep things in perspective because usually it's only our heads that blow things all out of proportion.

♥ Choose either to accept or to take constructive action.

Doodle, Scribble, Create!

1.   Doodle, scribble, create the steps you're taking and the behaviours you're changing to better accept you.

2.   Doodle, scribble, create the steps you're taking and the behaviours you're modifying to better accept a person or situation in your life that you can't change.

You Can Become Curious

Curiosity surely did not kill the cat. Curiosity informed the cat and gave the cat knowledge, wisdom, and information and made the cat stronger. Curiosity grew the cat, enabled the cat, and empowered the cat. And the cat came out of its shell and reached to the sky. It found confidence and belief in itself and it started trying new things. Curiosity made the cat realise how oppressed it had been and what it had been missing all its life. Finally it started living and feeling free.

Curiosity also reminds me of the book *Who Moved My Cheese?: An A-Mazing Way to Deal with Change in Your Work and in Your Life* by Spencer Johnson, MD. The book is primarily about change; however, to enable change to occur, the two little mice, Sniff and Scurry, must be, first of all, accepting of the fact that their cheese source has depleted. They must then be curious enough to find a new source of cheese. Unperturbed, these two little animals scutter around until they find new cheese.

Their indecisive little counterparts, Hem and Haw, however, experience quite a different story. Having ignored the fact that their cheese source was dwindling in the first place (as the four of them had eaten their way through it), and then become angry and enraged when the cheese 'disappeared', they closed their eyes to what was true and real, and they blamed the world around them for 'moving the cheese'.

Lap up information and observations, and embrace everything they can do for you and help you with. Information is your friend. And when I say lap up information, I don't mean watch the news every night; neither do I mean believe every single thing you read or are told. Be open, be curious, and form your own opinions about information you receive. Question and challenge your beliefs.

Search high; dig deep. Google different topics and scan your library shelves for books on subjects that interest you, tickle you, nudge you, or jump out at you – and even ones that don't. Ask questions, listen to others, and I mean really listen properly, with your ears and your heart, being silent, without interrupting or assuming what's going to be said or jumping to conclusions. Look at the courses available at your local college. Search online for current science discoveries, search for events, festivals, fairs, and expos that will be near you in the next six to twelve months and consider going. (What have you got to lose?) Google a variety of publishers to find out what's new for reading. Get distracted and go off on a tangent around the Internet and enjoy one thing leading to another, delight in what people are doing across the world, relish little tasters of what's going on. Again, I don't mean getting your information only from looking at news and media sites. In fact, on your curiosity mission, I'd suggest going out of your way to avoid media sites; they're telling you only what they want you to know. Either that or challenge what they're telling you. Get curious about how your news and media shows are dictating what you can know.

But mostly, just let yourself come alive!

> Be less curious about people and more curious about ideas.[23]
>
> Marie Curie

Going loose around the Internet can be procrastinating, depending on what you're actually there to do, but done at the right time, in the right context, with the right focus, it can be highly invigorating, incredibly energising, and very exciting. The Internet can open your eyes to opportunities you didn't even know existed, and there's nothing stopping you reaching out to try some of these opportunities. Nothing other than your ego. Nothing other than your head.

Consider trying something you've never tried before. Perhaps you've always said you weren't interested in classes offered at a local outlet or community centre. That doesn't mean you can't ever go or that you always have to remain 'not interested'. Often universities, colleges, public schools, churches, and community halls run free lectures and talks on a whole range of topics. Change your mind. Go on, change your mind about something. It doesn't give anybody the upper hand; it doesn't allow someone else to 'win' or to take a hold over you. It means you're open, it means you're curious, and it means you're willing to try. It means you're stepping outside your comfort zone, you're evolving, and, right now, at this time in your life, at this point in this book, that's exactly where I'd love you to be. Hats off to you!

Really notice through your day what makes you wonder about things. Jot things down, and when you get a chance, Google them or research them or ask questions of people about them. One thing leads to another. Whenever I find I have quite a strong curiosity or question about something, I do go out my way to find answers and information. Sometimes it takes some time to find clarity, but reading about topics when I get a few minutes helps to generate new and different thoughts and ideas in my conscious head; often it causes butterflies in my heart. It keeps me open and informed and excited.

> ♥ Open up to new experiences and new knowledge; they can open new thinking.

During the one year I attended university I used to sit in lectures listening, and wondering, *But why?* I'd get left behind because I was busier processing the bit I'd just heard, wanting to know more, than I was at keeping up with the constant stream of information coming from the front of the room. My friend used to say, 'Stop asking why. You don't need to know why!' This takes me back to the reasons I gave earlier that I didn't continue at university. I couldn't simply be a puppet rehashing the parts the institution decided I could know about, which included only the findings and opinions of others, never my own. I was not only discouraged from having any thoughts or opinions of my own, but I was marked down in exams for having them and sharing them. My curiosity has always been inspired, and I couldn't have written this book if I wasn't answering for you at least some of the 'whys' I know I would be generating if I were reading it myself. But I'm also leaving plenty of room for your own curiosity, research, and investigation.

Curiosity and becoming informed doesn't necessarily mean you like or accept or believe what you're reading or hearing. It just means you're collecting information. The more information you have, the more you can discern for yourself what you think or believe. It's up to you to decide whether you like something that you're hearing or not; the point is, having the information allows you to weigh up everything you know and proceed accordingly.

> But the biggest problem of map-making is not that we have to start from scratch, but that if our maps are to be accurate we have to continually revise them. The world itself is constantly changing.[24]
> M. Scott Peck, MD
> *The Road Less Travelled*

Doodle, Scribble, Create!

Perhaps something has arisen in the pages of this book that you haven't looked into yet but that you're curious about. Or there might be something that came up in your day, or something that's been niggling at you, or you might have actually been meaning to look into something in particular once you got the chance.

Doodle, scribble, create your findings as you give your curiosity freedom and space to enquire, research, and come alive. Go on to create a further flurry of colour representing the additional information you found, other interesting points or perspectives along the way, and wrap up with a display demonstrating how you're going to maintain curiosity and make it a part of your life.

Make this colourful explosion a part of your life.

You Can Think Big, High, and Wide

When I say think big, I mean think 'big picture'. Or, rather, think 'high'. Instead of thinking shallow, narrow, and blinkered, and according to the beliefs you've always had, think high, broadly, and wide open. Challenge your thinking, challenge your mind, challenge everything you've ever believed. Challenge the reason for the beliefs you hold, and use the universe – all that is out there for you – to help you to change your energy. This, in turn, will change the way you feel. Bad, negative, pessimistic, flat energy does nobody any good, least of all you.

Challenge yourself to see the positive side of things – the optimistic side of things. Just as it is with everything else, if that doesn't seem natural, it'll become more natural if you give it a chance to become natural – and if you want it to become natural.

As I write, I'm thinking of the number of people among us who are on some kind of antidepressant medication. There's something wrong about the fact that we're all feeling so down. It's surely got a lot to do with the fact that we've been listening to and measuring ourselves up against external sources for so long. We've been defining ourselves through our occupations, careers, and families; living our lives according to something other than our own true selves; getting stuck on past events. On the whole, we've been brought up to feel small, scared, and stuck in our place. Those who have followed their hearts, believed in themselves, and not compared themselves with others, or allowed status or the opinions of others to have a negative impact on their lives, have achieved genuine fulfilment and satisfaction.

❤ Follow what's inside *you* and keep on *your* adventure.

Some Western societies, or parts thereof, have a collective destructive tendency to stigmatise people who follow their hearts and pursue their dreams, or simply want to do better for themselves. I found this to be particularly rife in the corporate workplace. Individuals are – or certainly were – often condemned and resented rather than congratulated on their attempts to progress in their career or better their life. This tendency is known as tall poppy syndrome, and it basically describes a culture in which people who 'advance' themselves are scorned and tormented, often very subtly, either directly or indirectly, usually on an emotional level, by their colleagues and peers. Those seeking to progress while they are too busy listening to their egos over their intuition could be trampled beneath this behaviour.

Tall poppying happened to me around 2000–2001 when I was offered a leadership role over colleagues who had been in that particular work environment for longer than I had (some only a matter of weeks or months longer than I had). They viewed themselves more worthy of the role. I was shunned by a group of people in my work environment, to the extent that one co-worker would cross the road to avoid having to walk past me in the street.

Experiences like these are never nice experiences, but they're the ones we grow from more than the easy ones in which life's a breeze and everything goes our way. I appreciated the experience because I grew in strength and wisdom. This wouldn't have happened if everyone had been my friend.

I continue to 'throw caution to the wind' in different ways as I follow my heart and the truth of my own adventure. I'm shedding my dark suit of ego armour as I publish this book, create a website and a Facebook page, and take on the world in my own name. I'm consciously and gradually following my own bigger picture, being guided by my intuition and my heart, being gentle, loving, and patient with myself. And I am being very selective and objective about when I listen to my ego, or the opinions of others.

Listen to your heart. Your heart knows. My heart is telling me that I'm on the right track and that the doubts and concerns of others are doubts and concerns they have about themselves. They're not in my shoes. They don't have the benefit of my beliefs and my experiences and my reality. I must believe in *me*. I believed in me when people were crossing the road to avoid me all these years ago, and I believe in me now, fifteen years and many more life-on-earth challenges later.

You, too, can think high and stand tall. Listen to your heart. It's your truest friend, and it brings you a strength and confidence you don't have when you listen only to your head.

♥ Your heart is your truest friend.

Chat With You

Talk to your inner self. Chat with yourself as that best, most trusted friend. You don't need to do it aloud, but do talk, ask, listen quietly to what your higher self, your inner being, is saying to you. Tune in to yourself, and you'll open up to receive the answers. I discuss ways you can 'receive' in the next chapter.

Don't tell people you're talking to yourself, or rest assured they'll be at work with your ego, telling you you're nuts. And you're not nuts. I've talked to myself for years, even before I realised about the me inside and the me in my head.

While chatting with *you* may seem 'small picture', remember that what's inside is an energy that's linked with our universal energy. Chatting with and listening to *you* will help you to think big, high, and wide.

Talking and listening consciously to what's going on inside will help you to hear and feel your guidance system. When you start getting a bad feeling, or if you're looking for direction or support, ask yourself how you should proceed. You need to listen, and you'll need to ward off your ego self, which will continue trying to butt in all the time. Tune in *inside*, allow yourself quietness and attention, and you'll get the answers. The answers are immediate, coming much quicker than the answers that come from your head. When you pay attention, you'll be able to tell the difference.

In the early days of starting a previous business, I had just made what I knew could become a long-term client. My new client asked me to fly down to a meeting with her and said that she would reimburse me for the cost of my flight.

I was beating myself up about this as, although flights had got much cheaper, I literally didn't have enough money to get myself a return flight down to Melbourne, even though she was going to reimburse my travel expenses. I felt quite sick about this. I didn't want to tell her I couldn't afford the ticket; that just didn't seem 'professional'. I really didn't know what to do. My ego was tying me in knots. One morning I was cycling along to the gym and I asked myself what I should do. 'Tell her,' my quiet inner voice said. 'Just tell her. Be honest.'

Immediately, I got the whole thing into perspective, and it was in those days that I really started to accept that, if something's meant to be, it'll be. If it's not, it won't, and as long as I'm being true to myself and not trying to be anything other than me, then that will always be okay. I realised it was okay to be honest, that if the client didn't appreciate my honesty, then so it would be. That reaction would demonstrate more about her approach and expectations than it would about me, and the situation would progress in whatever way it was meant to progress.

I spoke to the client later that same morning. She paid for my flight – hardly batted an eyelid – and we became very close in our working relationship for a few years. Alaina was a gift – a strong, special, and amazing lady whose trust, faith, and belief in me was grounding and humbling. I continue to thank the universe for bringing her into my life. She will shine her light wherever she goes.

Listen to your feelings and your experiences. Listen to your heart. Listen to whatever it is you can feel going on inside. Stop listening to the external world and be guided by your inner light. It will tell you exactly if you're on the right path for you; it will tell you exactly if an experience is the right one for you to pursue or not; it will tell you exactly if someone is right for you at any given point in time.

How many times have you said or thought you should have listened to your gut?

♥ Believe in *you*. Trust in *you*.

Doodle, Scribble, Create!

Doodle, scribble, create one way that you're going to think big, think high, think wide, listen to your intuition, and chat with you. Challenge yourself to think differently about one thing that's going on in your life at the moment. Ask inside how you should pursue the next stage in the situation. Ask inside and listen to your guidance. What's your intuition telling you to do or think?

You Can Be Grateful

I discussed this in Part One, but it fits in nicely here as a reminder. Take a few moments to give thanks now. Feel blessed.

I remember walking to work one morning. For the entire twenty minutes, I sang my own words to the Levellers' 'What a Beautiful Day'. 'It's a beautiful day,' I sang. 'It's a beautiful day. Everything is perfect in my own life today. It's a beautiful day. The daffodils and the birds are in my eyes and in my ears today.'

And my song continued like that. I made it up as I went along based on what I saw and felt around me and within myself, till I arrived: 'It's a beautiful day. Thank you, universe, for my job. I'm about to go inside and I know everything's going to be okay.'

You get the picture. Thank you, universe.

Doodle, Scribble, Create!

Doodle, scribble, create five things for which you feel deeply blessed.

You Can Intend ...

... WHEN YOU ACKNOWLEDGE THE POWER AND energy of the universe and you see yourself as a connection to that power and energy.

... when you acknowledge the strength of the law of attraction and remember you have your own free will and can make your own choices.

... when you focus on love instead of fear.

... when you show gratitude and thanks for everything you have.

... when you open your mind, arms, heart, and soul to potential, ask questions, challenge, and review, and think big, broad, and wide.

... when you accept yourself and others and things as they are.

You're in a perfect place to set the intention to smile more and make more to feel good about in your days!

💜 You are ready to create.

The power of setting intentions and visualising outcomes cannot be underrated, understated, or shouted loudly enough. Opening your mind leads well into intention as the two start to overlap. But you need to be open to achieving your intentions for them to be worth setting.

You need to believe.

We've mentioned intent and intention a few times up to this point. It's one of the main points of this chapter, and it's about to become a big part of your life, if you'll allow it. Say hello to setting intentions (looking inside) and goodbye to unconscious plodding through whatever your day's decided to bring you (looking outside).

Now is the time to reverse the habit of a lifetime. Now is the time to tell your day what you'd like it to bring you, and decide how you'd like your day to go.

Setting your intentions is easy. But, as with everything else I'm talking about here, you have to do it consciously and from a place of love. You have to be quietly and positively accepting, and you must *believe* that setting your intentions will help you.

I have now read a lot of what I'm talking about in books, but I'd already worked much of it out for myself before I ever came across it in print. I didn't accept that some experiences could be as bad as my experience of them was, so I started looking at what I could change about certain situations. I quickly realised that, in every situation, the only factor I could have any effect on was me. I started to consider what I could do differently to change the way I approached certain situations, and how I reacted in some situations. Over time, I intended, visualised, appreciated, and looked at the universal picture, which helped keep my very small situations in perspective. I didn't always understand why I felt the way I did about some things, but some things just didn't feel right and some did. And that's been the basis of how I've lived my life – on how things have felt.

I've never understood people's absolute acceptance and willingness to be miserable. Not only do they let that attitude rule their own lives, but many pour that gloom over everyone around them. I've also never understood the willingness of the people around them to allow themselves to be consumed by those people's gloom either. I concede that it can feel easier to go along with or accept gloom rather than to confront gloom, but at the very least we don't have to 'buy into' or encourage the gloom. That is an example of responding with our ego, not with our truth.

In 1998, I was still thankful – two years on – that someone in Australia, on the other side of the world from Scotland where I had been born and grown up, had seen fit to offer me a full-time job. I appreciated everything I had, and I couldn't help but wonder what it was that made so many people in my work environment arrive at work so utterly miserable. Australia was supposed to be 'the lucky country', yet so many of my colleagues were in full bleak grey flow before they were even through the door, never mind had jackets off, lunches in fridge, and were sitting at desks. This tedious cloud of cynicism, sarcasm, and negativity was their daily lives. Quite to my dismay, many others fertilised this attitude, and I often felt not so much that I stuck out like a sore thumb, but that my roots were part of another bush, and I was an offshoot growing away in a different direction.

I couldn't understand why people didn't appreciate that they had full-time jobs. (See all references to 'thank you' and gratitude. This entire book could have been written quite relevantly under one chapter: 'Being Grateful'.) I didn't understand why, if they didn't like their job, they didn't do something about it. I was almost thirty years old and had never seen or experienced such an incredible concentration of negativity. I didn't know what they had that I didn't, or what I had that they didn't. I had no idea what was going on, but I couldn't, wouldn't, and didn't participate. As a result, I suppose I became used to kind of standing alone, if not physically, then spiritually and emotionally.

Having said that, I realise I was really only sticking with my values; in hindsight, I realise that's what I've always done. As a teenager, I was surrounded by peers who smoked, but I never took a draw on a cigarette. Since I was in primary school, if something didn't sit well inside, I've always said no. I learned early in my life that the consequences of not sticking with your values can be much more uncomfortable than sticking with your values, even in what can sometimes be a difficult situation. So it's important, now that you're clear on your values, to have the strength and belief in yourself to stand true to them. Live your truth and say no – and say yes to those butterflies fluttering inside your depths.

As you become your true shining light, you will live your true shining light.

❤ Intend your day with positive and clear feelings and images.

Just to finish the story, I was flicking through a new magazine one day, still back in 1998, and found myself reading an article by a psychologist who was describing exactly what was happening in my work environment. She was describing people I knew, and she was describing some of me. By the time I reached the end of that article, I had tears streaming down my face and had truly deeply identified with what she was calling emotional intelligence, or emotional quotient (EQ). I held on to that article for years, eventually applied to study psychology at university (although you'll have picked up by now that the reality of university wasn't right for me), and read every issue of that magazine until a few years later, when it suddenly disappeared from the shelves, presumably put out of print. I can only think it must have been too authentic or ahead of its time and that people didn't go for it. We have such a struggle in Western society accepting – or even trying – anything that's even slightly off main stream.

With intention setting, you can properly put some plans around your day. Set clear, positive intentions, and drop any resistance – the cynicism and the lack of trust and belief – and your days will continue to improve vastly. I talk about 'allowing' under 'You *Can* Receive'.

It's All About You – Not Them

When you're setting intentions for your day, do not have intentions or expectations of, or for, others. Remember, you have no power over others; you have power only over you. You can set an expectation for yourself that you will react differently or in a certain way to others, but you can't have expectations that others will or won't do or say things, because they still will – or won't.

Having said that, if you're living a more 'feel good' life, then you'll attract happier people into your life anyway, and those who upset you will still be there, but they won't be upsetting you because your outlook and whole approach will be different.

In my early years in Australia, as I was trying to settle, I found it very hard to make friends. This was something I had never experienced before. I would meet people, and they'd ask for my phone number. They'd say they'd call me, and then they never did. Initially I wondered if it was me. I certainly wasn't sure at times whether my Scottish accent was helping me or hindering me. So I looked forward to hearing from people I'd met and was disappointed on a number of occasions not to hear from them, or to feel snubbed if I managed to get their number and call them. I decided I needed to change the way I was reacting, and to do that I had to change the expectations I was having of other people. I had to look inside at what I could do differently.

My expectations of other people had always been that, if they said they'd do something, they'd do it. I'd never had any reason to consider an alternative approach until I experienced these disappointments. I chose to 'unlearn' that behaviour, those expectations. In order to protect myself from being let down any more, I decided I'd stop taking people at their word. I set down a resolution to expect nothing of people. Now, when I decide to do something, I do it, and I take it quite seriously. So, for a long time, I expected nothing of anybody, no matter what they said. I didn't become cynical and disbelieving. I was quite objective in the way I went about it. I just stood far back and away from what people were saying, almost closing my ears.

Funnily enough, I became so good at this that, when I met a girl who was to become a very good friend of mine, my smiling and patient reaction to her asking for my phone number was combined with a thought along the lines of *I'm no fool*. Although we'd hit it off at an open day we'd been at, and had a great time together, I simply didn't expect to hear from her. So when she rang a day or two later, I was blown away. I went round to have coffee with her the following Saturday morning and left seven hours later.

Don't set your intentions around other people's behaviours and activities unless it's in relation to your own reaction to those behaviours. You have no power over the behaviour of others; you have power only over yourself. You don't normally have to tread quite as extremely as I did on this occasion, although that approach certainly helps to diminish judgements you make of others, and it makes receiving anything an absolute honour!

♥ Expect things of nobody except yourself.

In a more recent and somewhat more everyday example, a woman sent me an angry e-mail at work saying how disappointed she was that I hadn't called her when *she had expected me* to call her. Yes, she actually wrote, 'when I expected you to call me'. Just as we can't change the behaviours of others, we can't take on feelings of guilt or responsibility for unfounded expectations others decide to have of us, or for any resulting accusations and complaints they choose to make. Many people aren't living with love and peace, but that doesn't make their misery our fault, even if they want us to be the source, or one of their sources. Nothing had been said or implied that should have led that lady to have had that expectation of me.

I used to have a poster in my bedroom when I was growing up. 'Little things are sent to try us,' it said. Funny, I just remembered that now.

The long and short of your setting of intentions is that you should expect things of yourself in line with your universal desires, your future, your truth, and your shining light inside. You should not expect things of other people.

In my twenty-minutes-walk-to-work job, I set my intention every morning, in the last five minutes when I was nearly there. I would intend – and *feel* – that, on the whole, my day was going to go well, smoothly, and with lots of smiles. I would intend certain things for various different situations or meetings that I knew I was going to be in, and I would also intend that I would get through 'x' amount of work.

As well as intending and feeling, I would also get as clear a picture as I could of my day and the different parts – even if it was only an image of myself breezing through it all with a smile.

Your intention for your day, occasion, behaviour, performance – basically for anything you've got to do or be – is yours. It should be whatever you want it to be. It doesn't have to be deep, long, or too fussy; it does need to be optimistic, positive, and heartfelt. You need to *believe* it will happen.

♥ Your day is yours. Intend to smile.

Doodle, Scribble, Create!

Doodle, scribble, create your intention for something specific on your horizon. Maybe it's simply tomorrow. Maybe it's the weekend. It could be anything: a meeting, an occasion, something you've got to do tonight. It doesn't matter what it is.

Intend positive outcomes, feel optimism, and picture and feel yourself at the event. Intend success for yourself at that event, and create what that success looks like.

Lesley MacCulloch

You Can Visualise

Intending is strong and effective, but combined with visualising it is *very* powerful. By visualising you *are* intending, but the two together, along with the right feelings and your belief in the combination, strengthen your power and belief and can have an amazing impact on your life.

Visualising is just imagining or picturing. When you are intending and visualising, you really do need to focus. It can help to shut your eyes. It's not a good time for your mind to be wandering. It's a few moments for you to properly pay attention to what you're thinking, and then to clearly intend and visualise what you'd like to happen in your day.

I'll talk through a few examples of my own because examples help to better demonstrate how you can apply these behaviours to your life.

I would say I consciously started visualising in 2005. I used to have a two-o'clock meeting every Wednesday on the eleventh floor of a high office block in Sydney. It was with senior managers and our human resources advisor. I was responsible for the national training team, which looked after the training needs of a thousand staff members. The attendees at this meeting were all stakeholders in a particular national learning and development project. I often felt emotionally battered after these project status meetings, having been ping-ponged from one side of the table to the other and back again, or so it felt.

I acknowledged that I didn't like the feelings those meetings evoked in me. So I considered what was true. I couldn't change the meeting, and I couldn't change the attendees or the project, but I *could* change how I dealt with my feelings, my perceptions, my reactions, and my approach to the meeting and its attendees. These things were within my power.

And so I began, each Wednesday, from the minute I got up in the morning until the minutes before two o'clock when I was in the lift on my way to the meeting, intending, visualising and *feeling* how that day's meeting would go. I knew that I was doing everything I could to progress my side of the project, that it was going well, and that I had nothing to fear from these meetings. I also knew that many of the others were simply trying to validate their importance, prove their worth, make themselves noted, and pander to their own egos and agendas. In order to do that, they often came across as questioning someone else's motives, and in those particular meetings, I was the target.

I knew and was very comfortable with my own motives and authenticity, so I realised that I could just be myself at these meetings instead of being scared someone would catch me out. In fact, they couldn't catch me out, as I had nothing to hide. If something had been delayed, then it had been delayed, and I reported on that. If something had been achieved on time or before, then I reported on that. I remembered that there was nothing to be taken personally; this wasn't about me, and it wasn't even about them. It was about reporting objectively on the status of a corporate work project. So I visualised very strongly and very clearly. I saw myself answering their questions and offering status updates objectively, factually, and without emotion. I saw myself taking nothing personally.

Wow! Those meetings turned around! I totally eliminated the feeling of dread I used to have. Intending and visualising turned my fear into fulfilment, empowerment, and strength.

💜 Intend, visualise, and feel — you're halfway there.

Jump forward a few years to 2009. I still visualised to a large extent, but I hadn't yet grasped the importance nor the *power* of using it, along with intention setting every single day. I had just arrived back in Sydney from the UK and was incredibly jet lagged, although I say that only in hindsight. At the time, I'd have said (and looked as if) I didn't know what planet I was on. Going through the bureaucracy and getting myself from plane to train with everything intact had taken its toll. I realised I'd lost my laptop.

At the time, I was running my editing business through my laptop, and although I've always been very good with the privacy of clients and their work, I realised that, if the information on my laptop got into the wrong hands, there could be issues.

Of course, nobody in an airport will watch your twenty-kilo suitcase in case you're carrying a bomb that somehow hasn't yet been picked up through thirty-six horrendous hours of flying, border controls, and baggage handling. I flew around that airport (ha ha – get it?) thriving only on panic – downstairs to the railway ticket section, down more stairs to the platforms, back upstairs to the airport arrival section. I can't even remember in what order it all happened, and it seemed like an hour, although it was probably about fifteen sweaty minutes. I had my backpack on, and I was pulling my twenty kilos upstairs and down, from east to west around the airport, trying to 'crisis think' where else I'd been.

On my way up in the lift from the train station back to the airport, I shut my eyes. I breathed deeply to calm myself down, and with every bit of will and positive visual energy I had, I called out to the universe to please, please, *please* help me find my laptop. I pictured and pictured and pictured finding it. As I was willing it back to me with everything I had, in my mind I received a picture of a young woman handing me the laptop over a counter. I held that vision until I got out of the lift, and then, somewhat more calmly, decided to go to the assistance desk ladies who listened compassionately to my messy explanation of what had happened.

I suddenly remembered I had put a luggage tag on my laptop bag that contained my name and phone number. I didn't have my mobile phone with me, as I used a spare one each time I was in Scotland, so I rang my partner to see if anyone had called my mobile, which was sitting in our apartment in Newcastle.

There had been a call! My laptop was at a particular café. I'm sorry I don't remember the name of the place. If I did, I'd give it a plug right here! As my partner said the name of that café, I focussed on everything around me, and what was I looking at? That same café.

I went up to the counter and began to tell the young woman there that I understood they had my laptop. Before I even had the words out of my mouth, she was handing it to me over the counter. I experienced the reality of my vision played out almost exactly as I had pictured it. Thank you to the young woman, and thank you from the bottom of my heart to the beautiful, honest, and wonderful person who found it and handed it in. May your light shine brightly.

Talk to the universe. Be guided by your energy. Trust, have faith, and visualise with one hundred percent focus, and you will find so many things in your life change.

Do it. Go do it right now.

♥ Believe it and you'll see it.

You Can Feel

All this intending and visualising is very good, but to amplify the strength, depth, and intensity of your creating, it's best to add some other ingredients. Sight and imagination are paramount, but do also make sure you can hear, smell, and touch things in your creation. What sounds can you hear going on around you in your picture?

What smells are there in the air? What do objects or people feel like in your hands. How do you feel inside? How does your body feel? Are you smiling? I always smile in my visualisations.

As well as all of this, you do also need to apply conscious thought; otherwise, nothing will change. Remember, we're dealing with conditioned thoughts and habits of a lifetime. They're not going to change overnight.

♥ Take back your power: become conscious about your thoughts.

But what's conscious thought got to do with a heading called 'You Can Feel'?

Well, until you're used to feeling and listening to your intuition, you'll continue to feel and listen to the thoughts coming from your head. Hence, it's important to become conscious – and creative – about your thoughts instead of just allowing your subconscious mind to respond as and how it will. Really *think* about what you're thinking – and saying – and gradually you will *feel* different.

Then you might actually change the way you feel as you visualise the outcomes you desire.

> I would visualize things coming to me. It would just make me feel better. Visualization works if you work hard. That's the thing. You can't just visualize and go eat a sandwich.[25]
> Jim Carrey

Doodle, Scribble, Create!

Using intention, visualisation, and positive-outcome feelings, doodle, scribble, create the outcome of something you are working towards. It can be anything: a holiday, a meeting, an occasion, an event, a date, this afternoon or tomorrow — anything. Be guided by your energy and trust. Have faith and create with full focus and positive belief the actual occurrence of that event. Include yourself, your feelings, and as much detail as you can. But remember to feel positive and believe. Take your time and allow yourself to flow; if you don't feel totally positive and believing to start with, the gradual development of your colourful creation will help these attitudes to unfold and flow.

Conscious Thoughts Can Change Your Feelings

First Things First

Let's get started with the minute you wake up in the morning.

What did you do to yourself in the first few moments – and I mean moments, not minutes. In the first few seconds after you woke up this morning, what did you do to yourself? And note those words – *What did you do to yourself?* Not, *What was the world doing to you?* That is not what's going on at all. What did you do to yourself?

Are you programmed, like I was, to immediately seek out yesterday's momentum and start the day with a groan, a frown, the dull thud of sleep? Are you programmed to sigh and start processing negative thoughts about your day, or yesterday, or both?

Catch yourself. Bite your tongue. Stop your 'here we go again' in its tracks. Stop your sarcastic 'what a great start'. Stop your doom and gloom comments and thoughts. Not only do they not work for you, they are not fair to those living under the same roof. Your mood can immediately bring them down.

Lie still for a few minutes and love your warm bed. Love your cosiness. Love the fact that you're protected by the four walls around you. Love that you've slept. See your morning with different eyes. Look for things you love. Love the man or woman, child or pet, the beautiful, blissful space around you. Love your haven. Love yourself. Love you. Love being alive.

Actually think about the morning. And what about yesterday morning? What did you do? What did you say? What did you think? What words did you say aloud to spark off your day and everyone else's day?

Mmm, it's okay. You don't have to say it aloud. But let's commit to getting that sorted out. Why not promise yourself that tomorrow, whatever you find yourself feeling, you won't verbalise it unless it's positive or neutral. Your tone of voice speaks louder than your words, so choose to be conscious of that too. Don't share your perceived woes. Don't verbalise them or display them. And even if you're saying something neutral, be conscious of not saying it in such an aggressive or woebegone way that everyone can tell your mood from your tone and therefore still be negatively affected by you.

💜 New day, new momentum, new start.

This is a good first step. Each day is a new day, and although you can choose what thoughts you want to think, a good starting point is consciously managing what you actually say along with the way you're behaving. When you consider what comes out your mouth – and *how* it comes out – you take ownership and responsibility, and you show your ego who's boss. You're shining your light from the minute you wake up. And if your light doesn't feel very shiny and it's not showing you the way by this time tomorrow, that's okay. It's not going to happen in the blink of an eye. Your intention will begin as a work in progress. Yoga is called a practice because even yogis and swamis and people who have done it their whole lives continue to improve and enrich. You're starting a whole new 'practice' so don't put unreasonable expectations on yourself. The habits of a lifetime won't change overnight. Take one step at a time, but commit to changing the way you think, the way you behave, and the words that you use – one day and one small step at a time.

💜 Consciously commit to your practice.

So, anyway, you've awakened, and you've managed not to think back immediately to what so-and-so said to you yesterday and how much you're not looking forward to whatever it is that's happening tonight. In fact, let's go as far as to say you're in a thankful appreciative place, warm and cosy, and happy enough to be there. You've breathed through your nose, all the way down into your tummy to let clean air and oxygen deep into your body, and then you've breathed out slowly through your mouth, and you've done that at least three times while focusing on the breaths. (I'm making assumptions! For the importance of breathing exercises, see next chapter, 'You *Can* Receive').

Nice work!

You'll get into something that works for you individually, but somewhere in that first hour or so of your day, you're going to intend, visualise, feel, and believe your day. You can do it right after you wake up, absolutely. Or you can start doing it then and finish it shortly thereafter. You might need to set the intention that you're going to manage to get up, get washed, and get dressed – and perhaps get everyone else up, washed and dressed – in the allocated time and without event. Try to keep your intention positive. Intend and visualise: 'My day will go well and everything will go smoothly'. That is more positive than saying: 'Nothing will go wrong'. Always put a positive spin on what you're projecting.

Don't use everyday normal events as excuses that it's not working:

- Did you trip over the clothes horse? Simply (and quietly and calmly) move the clothes horse so you don't do it again tomorrow, or else accept consciously that you knew it was there and just keep moving.
- Is your sock missing? Put on the light to find the partner, or put on a different pair of socks.
- Did you put your finger through your tights? Put on a new pair, or wear trousers.
- Did your son spill cereal all over the floor? Consciously acknowledge to yourself where this event sits in the scheme of your much bigger picture and quietly clean it up and keep going. If you've not got time for it, get up a bit earlier tomorrow.

These events are normal, everyday events, none of which is worth taking forward into your day, or passing onto anybody else's day. Deal with them at the time, keep them in perspective, and move on. Forget about them and mention them to no one. Put to rest the sort of non-beneficial, self-sabotaging phrases you use like *It's going to be one of those days.* Focus on keeping things in perspective, considering your bigger picture, and remaining positive. These examples may seem very small and very subtle, but they are highly powerful ways for you to live from your heart, maintain a loving, compassionate outlook, and listen to and live with what's inside. Changing the way you normally negatively react to insignificant events like these shows your ego that you're taking responsibility. This will discourage that voice in your head. And even if someone else tells you about how they tripped over the clothes horse, just smile or laugh. 'Ha ha ha! I did the same thing this morning!' Laugh. Keep life light. You might even help them get things into perspective!

Give focus and attention only to that which serves you well.

> ♥ Keep life light — give focus and attention
> only to that which serves you.

So, intend, visualise, feel, and believe that you're going to get up, washed, and dressed without trauma or event. Intend and visualise that everything's going to go smoothly. Set the intention that any hiccups will be skipped over and left as hiccups. Set the intention that *you* can accept rationally and deal objectively with anything, and that your ego is not going to make you upset about anything.

Intend your day at whatever point in the morning it works for you to do so. I used to do it on my walk to work. Now I usually do it either before I get up or while I'm in the shower. It might work for you to do it before you get up, or on your way to wherever you're going. If you're not going anywhere, do it somewhere that works for you, with focus, in the first hour of your day. You can get started in bed and then continue on your way to work, taking a bit more time picturing, feeling, and believing the results you wish to achieve.

I do want to make the point here that when I'm talking about 'work', I'm only using that as an example. This is about setting your intentions and picturing and feeling your day in whatever way that is relevant for you. No matter the details, the principle is the same.

You'll have realised by now that this isn't just about intending that things will go well. The package of intention, visualisation, feeling, and belief helps you to decide very generally what will happen in your day. Even more importantly, it helps you decide how you'll consciously manage how you cope with, react to, and deal with the events of your day. You're intending and picturing what you'll say, how you'll react, how you'll look and – here's the big one – how you'll *feel*. You might just picture a day going with ease. You might picture and intend your inbox being full of e-mails you can handle easily and that don't cause you grief. You might picture meeting up with all the other mothers and feeling empowered, assertive, capable, and beautiful. You might picture and intend that you go through your day with strength, confidence, and belief in your truth. You might picture and intend reacting to an annoying colleague or friend with a smile and a nod and feeling very satisfied about having been able to do that.

♥ The day is yours. Picture it.

Throughout the Day

So, you've woken up, you've made it out the house or you're in situ at home, you've got a clear picture, and you feel good about your day – *and* you've reached this point still smiling.

This is where it can get difficult, as you face the reality of your day. However you spend your days, try to make a point to employ conscious thought. Gradually look for ways and means that work for you to help you to remember to consciously bring *you* into your day and to help yourself stay conscious of what you're saying, what you're thinking, and what you're doing. Don't spoil your powerful intent by allowing your subconscious mind to take over your day.

Here I offer some ideas that help to bring you back to your conscious mind and your intentions:

- Carry a specific crystal to help you to remember to behave in certain ways. Amethyst could help you to remember to stay positive. Lapis lazuli could remind you to listen, remain true to yourself and speak your truth. Rose quartz could guide you from, and to, a place of love.
- Write a note for yourself to remind you to stop and take stock for a few minutes. Have a few short calming meditations in your phone that you can do at points during the day, although even just stopping for three deep concentrated breaths helps.
- Read power messages or confidence messages or belief-in-self messages. When you find good ones, store them somewhere where they are easy to get to. Listen to motivational audio recordings.
- Stop and take a few minutes time out. Do some stretches.
- Consciously visualise biting your tongue, catching yourself to ensure you don't judge or criticise or get involved in something that has no substance or depth or that is negative.
- Take a picture of a beautiful flower, a bird, a raindrop on a leaf – any point of beauty and nature that you observe in your day. It's time to pay attention so that you can stop and look back throughout your day at a bit of splendour and life that is bigger and stronger than any given point in your day.
- Go to the library at lunchtime and just sit and write in your diary or journal, read something off a shelf, or listen to something in your phone.

- Sit on a bench in the fresh air, shut your eyes, and do nothing but breathe and let thoughts flow in and out of your head. Thoughts will always come and go; it's choosing the ones on which you focus your attention that's important.

In his book, *Stop Thinking, Start Living: Discover Lifelong Happiness*[26], the late Richard Carlson suggested a technique that I have used successfully: Pay attention to your thoughts, and when you start to think something negative, catch yourself and state 'Dismiss these thoughts'. This method can work really well. When you dismiss thoughts, they can't grow, and when they can't grow you forget them. On really difficult days, when I lived near the coast in Australia, I supplemented my efforts by going to the beach and standing in the water, facing head-on into the big waves, my arms stretched out to the sides. The power of the waves as they crashed against me cleansed my head, my mind, my brain as I envisioned them washing all negative thoughts out of me and back in to the shore. This was an incredibly grounding and calming thing to do. Strong wind can work in a similar way. Use whatever you have in your surrounding environment to help you.

- Kneel on the grass and put your face and your hands in the morning dew. Close your eyes and breathe our wonderful earth, inhale the oh-so-natural smell of the soil, love the new day. Feel your connection to all that is.

The Quick Coherence® Technique I mentioned earlier is exactly the same idea as dismissing your thoughts; it's just a bit more recent and probably has a little more science behind it. The intention is the same – catching your negative thoughts before they turn into something that doesn't serve you, and using joy, love, and whatever makes you feel good to help that to happen and to focus elsewhere.

♥ Feel your connection to all that is.

It's hard getting started on the change of consciousness as you really are paying attention to your thoughts, your reactions, and your feelings all the time, or as much of the time as you can manage. When living in our subconscious, we tend to float along because we have let go of our power and simply accept whatever comes our way as fate, or our bad luck. Then, before we know it, we get all tied up in negative conflict, often without even realising that this has become our norm. And when good things come along, we accept them as good luck or a nice surprise, sometimes even thinking *What did I do to deserve this?* and immediately expecting good fortune not to last. Change your focus, pay attention to your thoughts, become more conscious – it all helps to change your reality.

Find a way to consciously put out carefree feelings and emotions. This takes effort. It takes focus and concentration and requires you to pay attention. If you start to feel negative emotions arising – which you will do frequently since you're changing the habits of a lifetime – actually consider why you're feeling what you're feeling. Challenge what it is you're getting anxious or frustrated about. Consider the reasons for your emotions, keep them in perspective, and then do something about them. Is your anger worth it? Is it going to change anything or is it just going to make you angrier as you wallow in it and allow it to play on your mind? What's the message in your anger? Take constructive action and look at what *you* can do to change either the situation or your reaction to it.

I talk a little bit more about this under the sub-section 'Acknowledge the Fear', which is coming up in a few pages.

❤ You deserve good fortune, earth child. Pursue it.

Doodle, Scribble, Create!

Think about today, or yesterday, or the last few days in your life. Consider what your reality was during that time, and then:

1. *Doodle, scribble, create how, with self-awareness, conscious thought, and concentrated effort, you could create better feelings and more loving outcomes the 'next time round'.*

2. *Doodle, scribble, create what different reactions and behaviours, generated from this exercise, that you will apply to your life with immediate effect.*

Acknowledge the Message in the Fear; Consciously Share Only Love

I remember lying in bed one morning. It was late; in fact, if I stayed there any longer, I would be late for work. I picked up my phone and set out to text a colleague. I typed out these words: 'This is draining the life out of me!'

Now, there was a bit going on there:

1. First, I had put into words the negativity I was allowing myself to feel about going to work. I was focussing my attention and hanging on to things that had happened in the past (at any point before that moment). All of this only served to validate those thoughts and feelings, which only then served to keep them coming.
2. Second, I was about to spread that woe – that negativity – to my colleague who, like me, overnight, had had the opportunity to cease the momentum of the previous day and wake up to a brand new day with a clear head. I was the one who was choosing to focus on negativity. I was the one who was allowing my ego to take over and affect my day before I was even out of bed. What right did I have to send someone something like that! Sending that text would put a dampener on my colleague's morning which, depending on where my colleague was at that morning, could then be passed to someone else's morning. This is how the swamp sucks us in and swallows us up before we've even had time to think a conscious thought.
3. Third, my negative action was only ensuring that, however I had been reacting to what had gone before, I'd react the same way again on that day.

My inner being yelled at me with love. Fortunately, I realised that what I was doing wasn't being done with love; it was being done as a result of some form of fear mechanism. The main things that needed to change were my attitude and my choices. For the sake of both my colleague and myself, I deleted my words and chose not to send the text.

As soon as you've gone that deeply into those sorts of thoughts – and it can take only seconds – you have to work twice as hard to get rid of them. I didn't leap out of bed that morning, but I did get up, get ready, and get on with my day. Although I wasn't singing 'It's a Beautiful Day', I did get to work that particular morning. I did also remember that it was my choice to be in that job. I consciously chose to stay in that work environment for the time being, and so I worked on my attitude over the next few days to make it feel better both for myself and for everyone I touched through the day.

Make sure you have friends you can talk to about anything. If you don't, try meeting new people in different circles and networks. Try new things and try doing things in new ways. Open yourself up to chatting with someone in the park or in a shop or at an event. You never know where or when you'll bump into someone who just 'gets' you and knows exactly where you're coming from. Once again, you've got nothing to lose and everything to gain.

We all have fear, and we certainly need to share our woes and have shoulders to cry on. There's a difference between sharing a negative and unnecessary text with a colleague and sharing some of what's eating away at you with a true and good friend. Do, however, become aware of the friends you're sharing your fears with and make sure they're friends who will help you to find the message in the fear and then deal with it objectively. You don't want to share with people who will feed your fear, help you blow your fear messages out of proportion and perspective, and end up making you feel worse.

♥ Be choosy.

Focus on Three Things You Love

Instead of lying there filling yourself up with misery and woe that you'll spread as soon as you come face-to-face with someone (or even, as I almost did, *before* you've come face-to-face with them!), spend those early moments of your day giving yourself a break. Try to maintain the clear head you've woken up with for as long as you can, and enjoy the reprieve. Breathe.

As you open your eyes and enjoy a few moments of early morning bliss, focus on what you've got in the here and now. Focus on where you are. Think about everything you *do* have and *can* do.

Focus on three things around you that you love. Breathe and say thank you. If you can't identify three things that you love, then put a new action on your to-do list: 'Get things I love around me'. From where I'm writing now, I see my healthy green peace lily plant; my candles; my crystals; the sky; and my wonderful friends the birch trees, outside the window. It's important to have things that you love within easy view and easy reach.

And if the sun is shining in the sky, that's a bonus.

♥ Beauty is all around you. You don't need to look hard.

Acknowledge the Fear

I've talked a lot about acknowledging the fear-based messages from your ego. The messages may not always feel like fear, as such. Remember, fear represents your negative set of emotions and bad feelings. Consider what your feeling of fear is about – what it's related to. Acknowledge it and accept it as a message. We accept messages of physical pain, so why not simply accept messages of emotional pain?

Yes, the messages can beat us up, drag us down, and drain us empty. We need to look the other way for only a millisecond for them to do that. We're tuned to negativity. It's embedded in our societies and cultures. Throughout our lives it's become embedded in *us*. It's not going to go away in the near future from the world around us, but we can detach ourselves from fear and turn it into positivity. We can change how we behave, think, react, and speak. And the most constructive way we can do that is by, first, choosing to become conscious about the thoughts we think, and then second, treating our negative thoughts as messages and being selective about what we do with these messages. If you asked me for a third right now, I would say it would be to consciously choose what you're watching, listening to, and reading in the media. Embrace your power, and be particular about what you receive and believe.

Practise focusing on nothing more than what the message coming to you is telling you. What is the source of your fear, your nausea, your nervousness, your worry, your embarrassment, your anxiety, your anger, your discomfort? Where is it coming from? How is it making you feel? And why? Can you define *why* you're feeling these feelings? There are reasons you get bad feelings or bad vibes. The idea is to notice them as they arrive so you can hear what they're saying and then do something about them without allowing them to take root.

As soon as you feel a hint of negativity, take steps to do something about the way the message makes you feel. Change it into something that feels better. If you don't know why you're feeling the way you're feeling, consider whether you need to know why; it may be enough to identify the feeling as negative and then move to make constructive changes to feel better.

The following are examples of questions you could ask yourself to help you define what's going on and how you can deal with a message and/or keep it in perspective:

- Does the reason for your fear relate to your beliefs about something?
- Is the message from your ego? Is your ego feeding you fear? Have you listened to what your inner voice has to say?
- Are your values being challenged?
- On a scale of one to ten, how rational is your fear? What would someone else's answer be to the same question? Sometimes looking at how someone else reacts can help us find perspective. I don't mean you should compare yourself with others; I just mean you should keep an open mind. We can become quite blinkered and imprisoned by our own barriers at times.
- Are your feelings about your fear helping anybody (including you)?
- What can you do about the situation? What can you change?
- Do you need help in dealing with the situation and determining where your feelings are actually coming from?

Let's use an example. Apply the questions above to the following brief scenario.

You fear you don't have much to offer, that everyone else is better than you at work, at being a parent, at living their lives, and you spend your days comparing yourself with others.

Now let's answer the questions:

- Yes, your feeling is related to your beliefs about your self-worth. You are comparing yourself with others and with what you see and hear going on around you.
- Yes, the message is from your ego. Yes, your ego is feeding you fear. Give your inner being half a chance, and it'll remind you that you have everything to offer; that you are just as good as everyone else; that we're all equal; and that you are worthy, beautiful, capable, deserving, and confident.

- Do you know what your values are? Are they being challenged? Only you can answer this one.
- Is your fear rational? This is exactly why it's sometimes good to enlist the help of a good, genuine friend who will tell you the truth. Even better, consult your inner best friends – your heart and your intuition – because they'll tell you *exactly* how rational your fear is.
- No, your feelings about your fear will never be helping anybody, least of all you.
- What can you change? In this particular scenario, you could work through the activities in this book to help you build your self-worth and love *you*.

And to address the final bullet point – quite possibly you do need help in dealing with the situation. Reiki is an energy-balancing holistic treatment that helps to balance the chakras. Chakra dancing is, perhaps, more fun and includes movement and sound that also help to balance the chakras. Deep breathing enables you to take the time to listen inside and cut out the ego. Guided and creative meditations enable you to reach high, regain perspective, listen to your inner being, and spend a few moments finding peace, calm, and harmony and remembering that you're worthy, capable, able, beautiful … and everything else that you *are*. Step into your power and take assertive action. Seek inside to encourage love and inner guidance over living in your head.

♥ Objectively and constructively address the message in the fear.

Analysing the messages in our fear can be difficult. We are complex beings, and it can be very tricky trying to define straight away what exactly it is that's going on. Often things aren't quite as they seem on the surface, and it can take a friend or a confidante, or just time, focus, and commitment, to help us dig deep and establish where issues are starting.

Often we perceive things or judge things in ways they're not meant; we all have so much stress going on that we take things the wrong way, say things we don't mean, or avoid saying anything at all in order to avoid potential conflict.

Hence, when we consider why we're feeling fear-based emotions about something, the answer can uncover something that's six times removed from what we thought were actually reacting to in the first place.

Dealing with fear can be both daunting and tough. But sweet heart, with patience you can emerge from your chrysalis and transform into the butterfly that you already are, fluttering inside. The hardest part is getting started and reconsidering your fear as a message rather than a way of life. Fear can play a significant part of your day and your life, and if you can be conscious of what it feels like in its various forms, where it's coming from, what it's telling you, and then take some steps to improve your world as a result, then you've achieved a big step and will be able to progress from there. As you recognise it and deal with it constructively, without engaging in the fear itself, you'll go from strength to strength. You'll gradually detach more and more from your ego, and you'll keep everything in perspective as a minor incident in the bigger scheme of your life and our amazing and powerful universal energy.

And you *can*.

💜 Live with perspective, confidence, and joy.

Doodle, Scribble, Create!

Think of a situation in your life about which you know you generate negative, non-self-serving thoughts that either lead to bad feelings or that you simply know aren't doing you any good in one way or another.

Take some time to analyse where the thoughts and feelings are coming from and why.

Doodle, scribble, create how you are going to use the message(s) to improve your world.

*Y*ou Can Receive

RECEIVING IS OPENING UP AND *ALLOWING* what you'd like to come your way. It means letting go of your hang-ups, expectations, doubts, and disbeliefs and just allowing your intentions, visualisations and feelings to come your way. It is allowing yourself to *feel* that you already have what you are seeking.

Just as I talk in these chapters about giving thanks, love, compassion, and appreciation, so too must you be able to receive these for yourself. We're aiming for balance.

I want to reiterate the importance of *feeling* and using your senses in relation to your intentions. If you set an intention but your head is still feeding you cynicism and doubt, then you're not open to receiving or allowing yourself to receive. In order to be able to receive, you first need to allow yourself to *trust*. Once you've set your intention, you're putting your faith in the universe and allowing it to bring your intentions and visualisations your way. All you need to do then is believe they'll come, trust they'll come, *feel* they'll come, see them, smell them, taste them coming, and allow yourself to receive them.

Easier said than done? Yes! Of course it is. Our heads are at work before we're even aware of it, often creating long-lasting and damaging effects. Just take it a step at a time, a day at a time, and above all, be patient with yourself.

Find ways to build optimism and a positive approach into your belief system. Your beliefs are profound, and you're likely to find they're quite cynical in how they guide you. Find ways to encourage your belief system to expect that things will go well. Tell your belief system to have faith, to trust, to live, and be alive!

Your process is to intend, visualise, and feel what you desire; believe in it; be open to receiving it (not cynical in your expectation that it won't happen); and expect and have faith that things will go well.

There are various practices you can adopt to help yourself allow, and they all require a degree of patience and time. Not a lot, but if you're used to a fast life, and all of this is new and you're trying to plant and nurture new seeds in your life, then they'll definitely need your commitment and focus until you build them into your life as a habit. You've already come a long way and are forming many new habits. Continue here just by making small conscious changes in your outlook, your attitude, and your conscious thoughts, of course.

As you're opening up and becoming curious, broadening your horizons and thinking bigger, you'll also open up to receiving messages and signs, not just from your intuition, but from your surroundings. We sometimes call these signs and messages 'weird' or 'coincidence' and laugh or explain them away, but as you become more connected with the energy within and around you, you will draw to you more signs. You can call these whatever you wish to call them – *serendipity* is a nice word for it – but as you open up to how universal energy can help and *is* helping you with your creations, you will also be more open to *receiving* these signs and messages for what they are.

♥ Open up wide and embrace.

Okay. What's she going on about?

Let's just say you're having trouble achieving something. That could be a message that you're on the wrong track and that you shouldn't spend any more time on it. That also links with acceptance. Accept that, if things are a bit hard, it might not be the right time to be pursuing that particular avenue. What feels more right? Are you being drawn in a different direction? Are you trying to swim against the tide? Are you forcing something that's not ready or willing? Are you resisting the message that's being sent to you? The guidance? If so, why persevere? Just leave it alone. If it's meant to be, it will be without your pressure or force.

This actually reminds me about my experience creating a website. I liked what I saw of a developer in another country. Although I wanted a developer geographically closer to me, I did really like the examples on this other developer's site. The only way to contact the developer with an enquiry was through the contact form on her website. I tried that one day, but the form wasn't working. A week or two later I tried again, but again the form wasn't working. Although I was starting to get frustrated with my weeks of procrastination over my website, and I had no inclination to do it myself, I took this as a sign that this developer wasn't for me. I accepted the message and moved on.

My acceptance that that avenue wasn't the right one helped clear my energy and open me up to what *was* to be the right one for me at that point in time. Moments later I was offered an opportunity to receive. As I leant back in my chair and asked the universe for assistance – *Oh where do I go here? Please, give me a sign!* – I looked over to the window, and beyond my birch tree friends was the most beautiful red setting sun. I typed 'red sunset web developer' in the search box and up came a local developer in Glasgow. I immediately got in touch, we met the following week – he was very curious about how I'd found him as at that point in time all he had was a placeholder page – and soon after I had my start-up website.

Pay attention, don't resist, and believe. You will receive!

Also, in the hour or two after I had handed in my resignation to a previous job, I walked past a bank where a huge poster hanging in the window yelled the word *liberated* at me in very big letters. I then entered a shop where I encountered shelves and shelves of Mars Bars shouting 'Believe!' at me. (Apparently the Mars Bars 'Believe' campaign was in support of England's World Cup football team, and not me, but hey, I happily received the encouragement!) If I was ever in any doubt about whether I was making the right move, the world was shouting at me that I was on track.

Don't ignore these messages. They are your guidance, reassurance, and confirmation.

♥ Really *feel* your depth, your capacity, your 'yes'.

You Can Breathe

I know, you've heard it all before. It's what hippies do, it's what people who meditate do, it's what people do at yoga, but it's not for you. It's boring. You can't do it. You don't get it. You've tried to breathe deeply, and you just don't see the importance or the value.

Well, if you can choose to review and leave behind that particular belief, you'll come on leaps and bounds. Indeed, if you get those curious juices of yours flowing and do some research, you'll find that deep breathing has scientifically proven health benefits. I meant what I said in the introduction – you're a bright shining being, and you're about to give more oxygen to that light. Deep breathing literally brings more oxygen into your body.

The fact that you didn't learn it at school, or anywhere else, before now doesn't mean a thing. Remember that to be clearly guided you need to keep revising your map. You've got nothing to lose other than 'Ego Negative' talking you out of things like this and putting down all your good ideas.

> The advice to 'just breathe' when you're stressed may be a cliché of Godzilla-sized proportions, but that doesn't make it untrue. The substance behind the saying is research-tested – and not only to manage stress.[27]
> David DiSalvo

Deep breathing is the *first* thing I offer to people who are looking to make small changes to ease their days. It is also *the* first step to opening up to receive. Deep breathing centres you and allows the hormone oxytocin to flow more freely through your body, and this helps you to be more receptive and to allow. You can't receive anything if your receptors are closed. You *can* do deep, calming, centring breathing anywhere, at any time, and it works wonders for your perspective. It also massages your organs, stimulates your kidneys and increases your vitality.

Even getting a taste of what breathing properly must feel like is amazing. I thought I understood the importance of breathing even though I didn't necessarily always stop and breathe deeply very often, but I'm only just beginning to understand the extent to which good, proper, focussed deep breathing can help your life. And three deep breaths is just the start. But it's enough of a start for here and now.

Most of the time we breathe down only as far as our chest. We're taught our whole lives that we need to be thin, so we hold our stomachs in and rarely, if ever, breathe all the way down and clear ourselves out. What were those things women used to wear? Corsets. Ouch!

On this adventure of yours towards ease and harmony, take time in your day to relax into your tummy instead of holding it taut all the time. Ideally, you want your tummy coming out as far as it can as it fills up with oxygen, and then deflating as you breathe out carbon dioxide and cleanse your inners of stale, stagnant energy. You might have heard this called breathing into your diaphragm, or abdominal breathing. They're all the same – deep breathing brings more oxygen into the body, and lets more carbon dioxide out.

If you're carrying out only shallow breathing into your chest you're not helping your stress levels, and you're not allowing that good clean new air energy down far enough into you for it to make any difference. All you're doing when you breathe into your chest is breathing for survival. Breathe deeper for quality of life.

> Shallow breathing limits the diaphragm's range of motion. The lowest part of the lungs doesn't get a full share of oxygenated air. That can make you feel short of breath and anxious.

> Deep abdominal breathing encourages full oxygen exchange – that is, the beneficial trade of incoming oxygen for outgoing carbon dioxide. Not surprisingly, it can slow the heartbeat and lower or stabilize blood pressure.[28]
> Harvard Medical School

Breathing properly brings in clean new energy from your surroundings, and given what I've said about energy and the universe, the point of that should be clear. You may have heard of Ayurveda, the traditional Indian mind-body system of natural health care, which focuses on the importance of breath – *prana* (life force) – as part of an individual's unique balance of health, physiology, and wellness. Until my teacher moved overseas, I attended a monthly chakra yoga workshop in which we would spend twenty to thirty minutes practising *pranayama*, a series of energising breathing exercises. You begin by clearing out old, stagnant breath from the depth of your tummy and go all the way through to breathing for balance and for organ support. I find pranayama deeply grounding, cleansing, invigorating, and balancing.

But don't worry. We're not here to attempt pranayama. I only told you that to make the point that breathing exercises are an aid to wellness and contentment. All I'm going to ask you here is to plant three deep breaths into your day as often as you can and as often as you think of it. For the time being, that will be quite sufficient to help you feel different and better.

The simple step to learning to breathe down into your tummy at all will be a huge step forward. Once you master and include it as a regular part of your day, you'll feel it gives you a similar feeling to having a weight lifted off your shoulders – at least that's what it feels like to me.

Be patient with yourself and expect to gain benefits. My friend started doing this the first time I mentioned it to her, and now she does it at work, at the bus stop, and at home. Three good proper deeps breaths will ground you, allow you to regain your perspective, and bring you back to balance. Deep breaths help you to stop reacting, or overreacting, and they help to calm you.

♥ Breathe deeper for quality of life.

The Deep Breathing Process Explained

So let's do it. Do it in front of your mirror if you can. You probably won't like it at first, but put your ego away and look at yourself objectively using the mirror as a useful resource to help you achieve what we're after here. Do whatever you can in front of a mirror because it will help you to accept yourself and your truth more quickly. It will help you see *you* rather than what you *think* you've been seeing all these years. That way you'll be in a far better position to see yourself objectively. Nowadays, even on a flat or unhealthy-feeling day, I can look in the mirror and like well enough what I see. It's a nice way to be. I haven't criticised myself in the mirror for a long time. Whatever physical or visual aspects of your life you're working through here, doing your work in front of a mirror while looking yourself in the eye will take you a long way forward.

Okay, the breathing process:

1. Release your tummy muscles. Yes, this alone might feel strange, so take some time to feel it and enjoy the sensation. It's wonderful. It's so freeing! Be still. Feel comfortable. Nobody's watching. Eventually you genuinely won't care if they are.
2. Breathe in through your nose nice and slowly. Put your hand on your tummy. You want the breath to reach all the way down into your tummy not just into your chest. As you take in a long slow deep breath, you can feel with your hand on your tummy if the breath is going all the way down or not. If you're taking the breath down far enough, your chest won't move very much at all, but your tummy will push out. This is why I sometimes talk about making a big tummy. You want it filled full of air, and it feels amazing when you really do this.
3. Make sure there's space between your shoulders and your ears. Stretch your neck tall and lower your shoulders. Make space for the breath to flow through you.
4. Once you've taken your deep breath in, hold it just for a couple of seconds, or for whatever feels comfortable, and then breathe out through your mouth slowly and steadily taking longer to breathe out than you did to breathe in.

Repeat the cycle two more times, each time trying to slow your breathing down just that little bit more.

Do this slow deep breathing practice as often as you can. You can do it standing up, sitting down, or lying down. As you get used to what it is you're supposed to be feeling, you'll be able to do it anywhere, whenever you feel you need it. I used to do it in the five or ten minutes before I arrived at work, towards the end of my walk to make sure I was calm, present, and at peace when I arrived. It was at that point, as I mentioned earlier too, that I set my intentions for my day at work and visualised how various situations and meetings in my day were going to go, along with what work I was going to get through. In my deep-focused breathing, I was setting myself up to allow my intentions to be received. I also believed I was going to achieve my intentions, and so I went off to work having filled myself with oxygen and decided my day.

Actually *focussing* on your breathing works in two ways: it helps you breathe properly, which in turn is cleansing and oxygenating, and it helps you stop focussing on other non-serving ego thoughts. And it's an easy thing to factor into your day – no excuses. The commitment here is remembering to do it. And once you remember, even if you practice it only once or twice a week at first, you'll naturally start to think to do it more often.

Please do the deep breathing. You deserve it.

> Deep breathing stimulates the main nerve in the parasympathetic nervous system – the vagus nerve – slowing down your heart rate, lowering your blood pressure, and calming your body and mind.[29]
> Sheila Patel, MD

Doodle, Scribble, Create!

*Choose something in your life about which you
have a concern or a decision to make.*

*Take three very deep breaths, expanding your tummy in the way
we've just discussed. Gradually slow down your breathing.*

*Touch your heart, close your eyes, and ask
yourself what it is you need to know.*

*Remember, your answer is what comes to you in that split second,
usually before you've even finished asking the question.*

*If you're not ready to run with what your intuition is telling you about
that particular issue (although that's what we're aiming for – your
faith in your own light), then ask it about another one, something
less important, and take action to follow the very original response.*

Doodle, scribble, create your experience of this and what it means to you.

You Can Believe

You do really need to *believe* that you can create what you desire in your life. This may sound scary or impossible, but if you think about what you've been getting in your life up till now, you may be able consider it as a possibility. You've got what you've believed – haven't you?

Basically when you believe you will, you will. And when you believe you won't, or even have a doubt, you won't.

Our hearts have super powers over our minds, so we must be able to *feel* inside what we want. We can tell ourselves all the stories we want from our heads, but if we don't *feel* what we want inside, then the results we're asking for will continue to elude us.

Now that you've come as far as consciously setting your intentions for your day – and visualising and feeling great results – why not then allow yourself to be prepared to receive these results? As with everything else we're talking about, you may not do this successfully the first time, but you have to start somewhere.

Our belief systems are powerful. Look at the habits we've formed over the years that we believe we can't break. Think about what's going on in your own head for starters. Look at the beliefs you hold about yourself and what you can and can't do, or how good you are or aren't. When you wholeheartedly believe that today's going to be another difficult, challenging, or miserable day so, in effect, you're setting that intention, and so you attract that. But, believe me, as you set clear intentions, *picture* situations throughout your day, *feel* situations and interactions throughout your day, you *can* turn that around to attract a great day in which everything goes well, or at least in which you cope with your reality and keep everything in perspective. Then, as long as you believe you'll attract that great day, and as long as you're ready to allow and receive that great day, that great day is exactly what you'll get.

Your feelings and beliefs are everything! Believe, feel the belief, and expect. Don't *dis*believe, feel the disbelief, and expect.

Feel the difference.

> ♥ You've believed you can't for long
> enough, so now believe you *can*.

The Importance of Positive Belief

Let's go back to the law of attraction for a minute – the law of *attraction*. This law works in such a way as to bring you what you're *attracting*. Ask, believe, receive.

I've talked about all of these steps at one point or another. Ask for what you desire. That's you asking, praying, setting your intentions, visualising, and *feeling* what you'd like. Put out there to the energy of the universe what you'd like in your world, remembering that your energy is connected to that universe.

Then *believe* that it will come. Feel and believe that your good day, your confident life, your world of truth will eventuate. Believe that the utility company or the broadband company will actually get it right. Difficult, I know, when your natural reaction is fury – but your deep breathing will allow you to open up, to calm down, to find your perspective, and, if you allow yourself, to *feel* the positive belief.

Just a brief aside: As you get better and more regular at your deep breathing, you'll find you can get your breath all the way down first time. Initially, you may have to take quite a few breaths before you can reach down into your depths. It can be like not 'getting' a yawn. As you open yourself up, in every way – physically, mentally, emotionally, and spiritually – everything moves and pumps better through your body, including your breaths, and you can breathe deeper more easily.

But back to what we were saying. Ask, believe, receive. Receive. That's the part we're talking about now – being open to receive. Allowing yourself to be open to receive. Believing you will receive.

The law of attraction likes us to live as if we already have what we'd like to have. The law of attraction doesn't like it when we focus on the lack of what it is we'd like to have. That means we really have to turn our feelings and beliefs around because it's those deep-seated actions and behaviours that determine whether we'll create our intentions.

The law of attraction wants you to have *positive* feelings and expectations so that you can attract your desires and intentions. Try to think of all of this in terms of energy, or picture a good, high vibration. If you're putting out positive energy and living at a high vibration, then you'll be drawn forward, pulled along, guided in the right direction. If you're stuck in a clump of negative energy, at a low vibration, you're not really going to be drawn anywhere. You're going to remain stagnant, enlisting more energy to become more stagnant. Pretend the universe is the pull of the full moon. Think of yourself as the tide on the full moon. Oh, joy! You're at your height!

Live, love, sing, be, and create!

Positive expectations are not considered presumptuous or arrogant – unless your behaviour in relation to them is presumptuous or arrogant behaviour. Negative emotions like arrogance, aggression, intimidation, and conceit clog you up and close you off from receiving anything other than more of the same.

The law of attraction can't work properly if you don't open yourself to receiving what you're intending and asking for. If you don't believe in or expect your positive intentions to manifest, you'll just get whatever willy-nilly experience comes your way depending on your energy and what you're feeling at any point in time. It can help to remember 'believing is seeing'. That's the power of our universe. Believing is the only way you'll receive what you're intending, as long as you *feel* and *believe* in your expectation.

Your feeling is so important.

Throw your arms up high, face the sky again, and breathe in through your nose oh so deeply. Feel yourself receiving. And breathe out through your mouth – aaaahhhhhh!

As I mentioned earlier, even just being neutral is better than being negative, so if it's too hard to believe and be optimistic, at the very least try to feel neutral about your intentions. That way you're still likely to have pretty good results, and it'll then become easier to believe.

❤ Believe and receive. Breathe in — believe
and r-e-c-e-e-e-e-i-i-i-i-v-e.

It's All in the Attitude

Some of you may say this is all rubbish. I'd like better workdays in my life, and that's never going to happen. Well, you can trust that, with that attitude, with that negative belief system in place, you will be assured of never having better workdays. So let's look at it the other way round.

At the moment, you're getting in your life what you expect to get – some good, some bad, most of it pretty accidental. You expect things to be tough, you believe things are tough and – hey – things are tough. You expect a difficult meeting and – hey – the meeting is difficult. You expect someone to annoy you and – hey – the person annoys you. You expect, you believe, and you get.

And funnily enough, we accept all that negativity. We believe it will be, and so we accept and *receive* it, often with a hearty welcome and open arms.

Oh yes, of course sometimes things go better than we expected. That could have something to do with the fact that we haven't focused solely on them going badly. Perhaps we found 'neutral' for a period and – hey – we get above average!

So why should all of that not work the other way round! You expect to have a day where everything goes smoothly and well, you believe wholeheartedly that you are going to have a day where everything goes smoothly and well, and – hey – your day goes well! This is because your attitude, your approach, your outlook, your emotional framework, your mind, your heart, your light, your soul – *you* – have all conspired to ensure that whatever happens, *you* are in control and that you react quite differently to the way you normally do.

Imagine living such a lightweight life!

Just think: the same things don't annoy you half as much when you're in a good mood as they do when you're in a bad mood, do they?

I mentioned Dr David Hamilton earlier. Dr Hamilton used to work as a scientist in the pharmaceutical industry, and when he realised he was getting more or less the same results, if not better, from placebo drugs as he was from chemical drugs, he left the industry to research, investigate, and write about scientific findings relating to the power of the heart, the power of the mind, and the power of love, kindness and compassion. He has since written at least half a dozen books, many of which discuss scientific findings proving the strength of our belief system. During a recent talk, he related a story about dementia and morphine. A person with dementia might require twelve milligrams of morphine for a certain treatment, whereas a person *without* dementia might need only six milligrams for the same treatment. The minds of the people *without* dementia are still working properly. Because they know they are getting morphine, and *expect* it to help the pain, their minds manage half the pain.

Dr Hamilton shares a story from the mother of a little girl who had a very itchy face from her chickenpox:

> She asked her daughter to go find a teddy bear whose face tickled as much as hers. When the little girl returned with a teddy, her mother told her that she should scratch teddy every time her face became itchy and that it would help stop her own itch.[30]

The little girl scratched her teddy's itchy face and the itch on her own face reduced so much that she didn't scratch her own face at all after that.

That's the placebo effect: attitude, visualisation, and belief. You have an extraordinary amount of power. All I'm doing throughout these pages is offering you ways to change the balance of your power and to focus it in ways that serve you. If you listen to some of Gregg Braden's talks, you'll learn more than just the Harvard University study I mentioned earlier – the one that found blood pumping around the foetus of a chicken *before* the heart had even been developed, which suggests that our hearts are much more than just organs that pump blood. You'll find there's an ever-increasing amount of research and information becoming available on the heart–brain connection. So if you choose only one area to keep an eye on, this might be a good one!

And if that's not enough to encourage you to carry out your own investigations and challenge your belief system, research Dr Joe

Dispenza and see what he did in 1986 when he was hit by a four-wheel-drive SUV, broke six vertebrae, and received a diagnosis that he would never walk again.

I'm no scientist, but I've been listening, learning, and absorbing, I've been challenging my thoughts and beliefs, trying new ways, and changing things in my life for years. I'm highly excited by the truths and proofs science and research continue to uncover and discover. I'm delighted I'm finding myself able to rid myself of a migraine through conscious focus, deep breathing, and meditation and that keeping an eye on my chakras is helping to keep me and my life healthy and well. Your world may not be what you think it is. Your attitude is based on what you think you know, and what you believe at any given point in time, so that becomes your world. What would happen to your world if you changed your attitude even just a bit?

♥ Open your mind, your heart, your attitude, and change your world.

Doodle, Scribble, Create!

Doodle, scribble, create how you are creating more positive beliefs and changing your attitude to life, things, people, and information. Create generally or choose something specific you're focusing on turning around. It could be a belief about your body, food, money, someone you know, or it could just be your general outlook on life that you know could be improved to serve you better. Commit to returning to this exercise for five days to create your daily successes, achievements, and progress.

You Can Let Go

I've mentioned elsewhere the difference that letting go of some negative things can make to your life. We carry around burdens, some of which are very personal and very painful, and some of which are trivial, minor, and, oddly, part of our comfort.

The trivial, minor ones need to go. Ideally they should all go – or at least be let go of. But if you can drop some easy weight now, other weighty areas will become more accessible and more manageable as a result. If you're already heavy with a burdensome load of things that don't *need* to be done, drop some of them.

I hear you: Define *need*. It's different for everyone. What you think 'needs' to be done, others don't, and vice versa.

Consider things as either essential or not essential. Consider things as urgent or not urgent. Consider things as important or earth shattering – or not important and not earth shattering.

We get bogged down in the unimportant areas of our lives for some reason. And in so doing, our stress levels and fear-related 'stuff' increases. We forget, if we ever knew, what it was we did when we had 'free' time without a page-long list of things we 'need' to do.

De-clutter our lives and our heads – that's what we need to do.

💜 Colour your life with things that make you smile.

This story I tell from experience:

I used to have a thick, burdensome, three-sectioned notebook, one section of which contained my ever-growing list of things to do. I won't even go into what the other two sections contained.

At one point in time, sadly, I had been proud of this notebook, which held an up-to-date list of everything I had decided I had to do – major and minor – as well as many papers and items which I'd decided needed to be reviewed or addressed in some way. (Oops, there's a give-away on what was inside one of the other two sections.) It was as if I defined myself through this horrendous book of chores, and I carried it everywhere.

So, as part of my own spiritual reconnection, having realised my resistance to my to-do list and the clutter it brought to my life, I decided to change it. I went through it and pulled out any task that wasn't absolutely essential to my life, and I removed all tasks that were there because they would be necessary only after the completion of a current task (yep, you read that right, I had listed – invented! – future tasks that I had decided would eventuate from completion of a current task!)

I also set an intention that the essential tasks that were reliant on an external party doing something would all be completed by a certain date. I know I've just told you not to have expectations of others in your intentions, but this little exercise helped me to get these tasks off my list and to at least be *willing* their progression instead of carrying them around on a to-do list when I couldn't actually do anything with them anyway.

All I left on the list were tasks that I was in control of and could complete myself. I also changed the name of my list. I overhauled my 'everything I need to do' notebook, got rid of all the bumf I was carrying around with me everywhere I went, and I called my new little *page* of things to do my 'friendly reminders'. Every single thing I now have on that list is a friendly activity like booking yoga or writing to a friend. It might be something I need to do when I'm out next, which isn't always exciting but it keeps the list small. This new arrangement keeps everything minor and keeps everything in its place. Because my list contains only 'friendly reminders', I don't even look at it from day to day. I usually just check it from time to time. Sometimes I forget things; often I don't bother doing things that, at another time in my life, I might have spent a lot of negative and heated energy on, only to achieve very little. Sometimes I can't even find where I put my list! Nowadays I mostly accept what is and spend my time and energy on things that are more meaningful and more important than having a menial chore that relies on another chore that will no doubt conjure up another chore. And if I forget something, I do it when I remember. My life hasn't fallen apart; indeed, my life has become so much lighter, breezier, and richer.

Life is for living. It's so easy to lose all perspective on this.

Challenge yourself to turn your back on things that you don't need, that don't need you or that really don't even need to be done. It's nice to help out, but if it's draining you in the process, then it's time to consider everything in your life and reprioritise what's really necessary. Think important, essential, or urgent. Where does a task, or a committee membership, or a shopping trip sit in the scheme of your whole life? What will actually happen if you don't do it? If you don't do it, will your world fall down? If your answer is 'No, but …', then think about why you're resisting.

♥ Does that thing really matter? Does it *really?*

We decide that things *need* to be done, but often it's far more empowering and satisfying leaving them alone and moving on than it is getting bogged down in the misery and perceived necessity associated with the chore. Usually it's only our head that's telling ourselves that x, y, or z needs to be done, and if that's the case, and nothing in the world will fall apart if you *don't* do something, then take it off your list. It's just dragging you down, eating you up, adding to your heavy load. My friend has a small section of her kitchen wall painted a different colour to the rest of the kitchen. It bothers her a lot – but when I walk into her flat I feel so at home. If

I even take notice of the wall, I don't consciously acknowledge it as anything other than character. Life is for living, not decorating. It's her space, her home, and her harmony. Sometimes the pressure we put on ourselves is a reflection of the judgements we feel we'll receive from others. Those friends, again, should perhaps be reviewed. A friendship is about the two of you, not what your house looks like.

Free yourself! Removing items from the list doesn't mean you won't ever do them; it just means they will stop ruling your life. Really stop and consider why you're spending so much time doing some of the things you're doing, and colour your life with things that make you smile, breathe more deeply, and feel much lighter.

♥ Love your kitchen walls! Be proud of your kitchen walls!

What's Not Essential to Your Life? (Be Honest)

My notebook-cleansing activity derived from the feelings of resistance I was experiencing about everything I 'had' to do. And even though I also set the intention that tasks other people were responsible for (solicitors, for example) would be completed by certain dates, that did actually happen, although I did generate a few communications outlining my intentions to those parties, which helped.

Also, as you're determining what tasks you feel are essential, ask yourself why they're essential. Why do you consider each of those tasks to be essential? We hide behind lists, chores, tasks, and busyness. They're all good excuses for avoiding – not having to address – other areas of our lives. Challenge your beliefs and your thoughts. Why do you believe that task is an essential task? Will you enjoy doing it? Will you feel satisfied having done it? Will the world end if you throw that task in the bin and forget about it? If that task were not on your list, would you breathe easier and feel freer?

Non-essentials are things that don't matter in the bigger, non-material, non-self-serving scheme of your life. We *like* to sound busy. For some reason, in our Western societies, we don't feel acceptable unless we're always busy, always doing something, always on the move. Yet doing nothing other than getting in touch with *you* is one of the most relaxing, blissful, and empowering things you can do. It is empowering because, when you take time out to *feel* and listen to what's going on inside, you are able to see the things that aren't working or don't matter; you're able to see clearly where you need to go on certain things and you have a chance to switch off your head and allow yourself to be guided by *you*.

♥ Let go, feel free, and live your life.

Doodle, Scribble, Create!

Think honestly and constructively about what you have going on in your life. What bogs you down? What jobs, tasks, and chores do you really not look forward to doing? What can you leave behind right now?

Look at your current 'to-do' list and highlight only the things that are essential. Pretend I am looking over your shoulder.

Now do it again. Really rise to the challenge and be strict with yourself. Mark only the things that are essential. You're not hiding from anything here, so now is the time you're going to discard the non-essential tasks from your essential list and from your life.

Now burn or shred or tear up that piece of paper.

On a whole new pad or page, using colour, create your new 'friendly reminder' list.

Make this latest colourful explosion a part of your life.

Doodle, scribble, create the thoughts and feelings you had when you carried out this task. For some it will feel like a very freeing journey.

You Can Allow

When things feel difficult, it's because our egos plant resistance in our way. I want to paint the picture of resistance so you can take steps to ensure it doesn't hold you up or get in the way when you set out to achieve the results of the intentions you are setting.

❤ Resist the resistance – open up to receive.

Resistance is what I was demonstrating when I didn't get offered my 'perfect opportunity' back in Part One of this book. Resistance is the guard I put up when I nearly texted my colleague with my moaning and groaning. Resistance is what was filling me up with gunk in relation to my burdensome 'to-do' list.

Resistance is the behaviour you're enacting when you push something away from you through your focus on its absence or lack in your life. Resistance is what I'm doing when I'm procrastinating and listening to my ego. Resistance is what holds you up. It's one of the hurdles your ego puts in your way when you're trying to move forward with positivity and lightness. Resistance is heavy, and it weighs you down. It comes in different forms including feeling doubt, frustration, anger, weariness, emptiness, and being put upon (often by ourselves).

Being open and allowing so you can receive opportunities that come your way is where you want to be. That's going with the flow. Remember back to when Vanessa offered me *Conversations with God* back in Part One? Thankfully I didn't resist too hard; I believed and trusted that Vanessa was offering me something for my own good, and I was open and allowed myself to receive it. I also allowed myself to receive the message inside the book – so much so that I bought a copy for myself and returned Vanessa's book the following week.

Many of us live almost permanently with some level of resistance. It is like a shield; it stops us from being in a position to believe in ourselves and receive our desires. Resistance is like a guard dog who ensures that nothing that's good for us gets through. It stops us from hearing our inner selves, and it prevents what we wish for from arriving.

Remember the example I shared about my 'perfect opportunity'? I decided I wanted that job so much that my whole thought process and demeanour was resisting it. Resistance includes *wanting* and *needing* because, when you want something, you are making the statement that you don't yet have it. I *needed* that job to get me out of the one I was in, not because it was really what I wanted to be doing. The law of attraction will bring you what you're asking for, remember, but it wants to *feel* your joy in already having it, even before you do have it. The law of attraction doesn't listen to the words – words are a human invention – it just feels your hardship energy so it gives you more hardship. And because you're used to hardship, you don't do much about changing your focus on your life; until now, that is, when you started to realise everything you have to be thankful for and started to offer up thanks on a daily basis.

♥ Ego helps us to resist; heart helps us to allow and receive.

When you feel resistance, throw those hands to the sky, close your eyes, breathe deeply, and honour your senses, your freedom, and your belief in yourself. You are an open individual, and you *can* come through this. Once you've done that, once you've spent those few moments allowing your perspective to change, and finding a more feel-good place, once you've challenged your mindset, you can have an objective think about *why* you're feeling resistance. Only then can you take steps to change the situation or your focus and perception.

When you need an answer to something, no matter how major or minor, the answer is inside you, waiting for you to allow yourself to receive it. The answers and the guidance are inside us, but we are closed and don't allow ourselves to receive them or accept them. We respond with our heads, with resistance. When our intuition speaks to us, it starts telling us the answers to our questions before we've even finished asking them. What comes in the seconds after that is our egos – our heads – answering. You will then almost immediately generate reasons for not attending to your concerns the way your intuition advises.

As you open up and allow yourself to receive, and get more used to doing so, you'll really hear and feel your intuitive answers more clearly. Your ego will slow down and not have as great results as it used to have.

> Remember it's the *still* small voice. We have to get quiet enough
> to hear it.[31]
> Mary Manin Morrissey in James F Twyman's film
> *The Moses Code*

Meditate

Yes, the importance of meditation is on a par with the importance of breathing. I know, it seems everybody's talking about it, but it's such a hippy 'om' thing to do that it's not for you. In fact you *can't* do it! You can't stop your thoughts. It's just a fad.

It's easier and more convenient for you to deride it than it is to try it. You hope it will just go away.

Yet, just as it is with breathing, scientists are finding more and more evidence for the benefits of meditation on our health and well-being. Indeed, many scientists are the ones spreading the word, and meditation teachers are working in corporate environments, schools, and also with veterans of the armed forces and their families to try to reduce stress and increase internal harmony.

As humans, as a result of the teachings of the societies in which we are brought up, we knock what we don't know, what we're scared of, what threatens our comfort zones. We prefer to stick with what we do know, no matter how uncomfortable that makes our lives. We've tended to deny anything moderately 'Eastern' or 'mystical', but in this case it seems the world is talking about meditation for all the right reasons. Encourage your newly enquiring mind to open up to the opportunity to try things out and find out what works and what doesn't work for you.

You don't have to look far to find a plethora of types of meditation. Some experts suggest we should be choosy or particular about meditations we practice, but if you're going from not having meditation in your life, to having meditation in your life, then I say just experiment and choose which types you like and which types work for you.

You can take courses in how to meditate or, like me, you can just enjoy the peace and quiet and see if you can establish some level of just getting yourself into the 'present'. As a beginner, the silence, the time out, the chance to allow your thoughts to flow and your attention to focus on something other than your daily stresses and tasks is a great start and will certainly benefit you. There are beautiful guided meditations available. When I was starting out, I found these were good distracters, and they helped take my mind away from its busy-ness. But you can try many and see what helps to take you to a place of calm and serenity. Find ones that suit you and work for you. Meditation should be enjoyable, relaxing, and easy.

Let's get a little bit of discussion (albeit one sided) going here:

- Meditation is about allowing your thoughts to flow in and out of your head with ease, focussing your attention on your breathing or the journey you're on if you're doing a guided meditation. In a guided meditation, someone talks you through a journey, sometimes to calming background music. You can relax into the imaginary journey you're on, which can be rather beautiful and highly blissful.

- Meditation can be as long or as short as you want it to be. You might want to take several five-minute calming meditation breaks at different times during the day; you might enjoy sitting for half an hour or more at other times. It's totally up to you.

- Meditation is deeply restful and can be done sitting up or lying down. It's about remaining conscious while allowing your mind to rest and move to a different, more subtle, level. Your focus can be on music, sound, vibration, your breath, an object, an imagined object, a part of your body, a guide, or silence. Or it can be a mixture of all of these. As you reach a deeper level of rest and calm, you will open up and more easily hear and receive your heart, your inner voice.

- Meditation is what you make it; however, it is a period of rest during which you focus on something other than your thoughts and stresses and 'allow' yourself just to be in a state of calm. Through that state, you become more conducive to 'receiving' your inner guidance.

- It is very good for you. Meditation, compassionate thoughts, love, calm, and time out enable your pre-frontal cortex (at the front of your frontal lobe) to grow thicker, which can help you to age more slowly, sleep better, and have a calmer more positive approach to your day.

Meditation really helps you to listen to your heart. It is the best way I have found to really *allow* the messages coming to me from inside to be heard. Meditation is like guidance; it's a 'switch off' time that allows what's inside to come to you.

Meditation is all love. There is nothing at all to fear. It's still, it's calm, it's relaxing. You can just 'be'. You still have all your thoughts. You are still in your body. You're just spending some regular time seeking a place of pure rest, focusing on something beautiful, something perfect, something other than your everyday realities, your ego, and your head.

You can find a lot of meditations, both free and for sale, online, and you can also buy CDs in shops. You can attend local meditation groups. None of these sources forces you to be or see or experience anything other than what you are, see, or experience. At the little group I go to, sometimes some of us have had a challenging week in our ego heads, and it takes a bit of time to reach a place of rest. After less challenging weeks, we might achieve rest more easily. There is no competition. There is no grading. It is about you and your comfort and inward expression. Indeed, from my experience, meditation and spiritual groups are the most accepting, loving, trustworthy, and supportive groups of people I've ever been involved with.

You *can* find time and you *can* make time – if you want to. Use part of your lunchtime to meditate. If you have a driving job, stop in a lay-by for five minutes and take time out. Meditate after you wake up, before you get going for the day. Commit to it. Set aside a time in your diary. We all have time if we want it. If this thing's important enough to you, if making your life more relaxed and that bit easier is important enough to you, you'll commit to making time in your day to meditate. It's simply a case of reviewing your priorities and fitting it in. This has become more essential to my friendly reminder list than anything that was on my chore list before. My next goal is to have it as a habitual part of every day, with no reminder necessary.

Meditation really does help to keep everything else in perspective.

> And through spiritual practice of prayer, lowly listening and meditation, after a while we are able to tell the difference between the voice of one of the constellation of shifting identities, or the true voice that's coming from your soul that wants you to be great and the definition of greatness is your capacity and your willingness to serve.[32]
> Michael Bernard Beckwith in James F Twyman's film
> *The Moses Code*

Sitting or lying down for a few minutes of proper body- and

soul-nurturing breathing and zoning out each day isn't a lot to ask for in the bigger scheme of things. It's not selfish, it's not boring, and you deserve it. But you do need to be open to what you can receive from meditation; it's not just lying around having a rest. It's pure, focused time. Set an intention for what you want to achieve during your meditation and then breathe, and allow yourself to go, flow, and receive. Otherwise you'll likely find yourself just sitting there waiting for the time to pass.

There are no excuses for not looking after yourself and helping your life to feel easier.

And no 'ah but's ...' Meditation helps you to find your answers and to receive your guidance – that quiet tingle, those butterflies, that wise source deep within. It's time to stop making excuses and start living, free bird.

♥ Breathe, relax, allow, flow, receive.

Doodle, Scribble, Create!

Find yourself a half-hour meditation. Look on YouTube, borrow a CD from a friend, or go to a class or group. You might already have recorded music or other sounds you know you can use. Decide whether you want to simply focus on your breathing, or whether you want a guided meditation or to listen to sound or vibrations. I like shamanic drumbeats. This is just your starting point; you will find what works for you. It might take you a few tries to find something you feel you can rest to for half an hour. You might just focus in silence on an object, an imagined object, or your breathing.

Intend that you are going to have a deeply relaxing, fulfilling experience. You might also want to put a question out to the universe that you'd like answered – that's up to you. You don't always have to have questions, but it can help bring clarity to something if you set your intention.

Allow yourself to relax deeply into your meditation for half an hour, and when you are ready, doodle, scribble, create your experience along with any messages you received.

Be

The first time I properly realised what 'just being' really meant was when I was sitting watching small finch-like birds in a tree in outback New South Wales. It's when you lose sense of time and you are totally absorbed and at one in the present. Your mind is nowhere else, thinking about nothing other than the beauty and sublimeness of 'now, this minute'. I've since realised I 'just be' quite a lot, and it's the most grounding, satisfying, body-and-mind-quietening activity I can think of doing.

When you're in the present, you're not thinking or worrying about anything else. Of course thoughts come into your head – thoughts always do. But they also leave. As in meditation, thoughts come, thoughts go, thoughts change, thoughts flow. If thoughts aren't receiving focus or attention, they have nowhere to go so they don't take hold and distract you or upset the moment.

'Just being' is when you're totally happy and at ease. You're totally happy and at ease when you're not focussing on what else it is you *should* be doing, or beating yourself up about something on your horizon. When you're 'just being' you *shouldn't* be doing anything else other than 'just being'.

I realise that 'just being' is what I do when I walk into a library. Libraries sweep me up the minute I walk through the door, and time stands still. I get totally absorbed in the environment and what's around me, and I lose all track of time.

When you practise breathing and factoring minutes and longer periods of silence in your days, and when you really appreciate the natural world around you, and when you stop putting expectations on yourself and comparing yourself with others, you'll be able to enjoy – you'll value – spending time just being.

Listen to silence. Actually listen to it. There might be a hum of cars somewhere, and sounds of birds, rivers, natural life. But actually listen to and feel the peace. Absorb it. Inhale it. Swallow it deep into your body.

💜 Be with your inner stillness.

Sit with your pet for a while just stroking it and enjoying feeling humble.

Watch the sky, the moon, the trees, the flowers – watch anything. Allow yourself to enjoy the present. It's deeply fulfilling, calming, and peaceful.

You don't always have to be *doing*. Create harmony by just being.

You *can* do this. It means sitting and enjoying the present moment for what it is. The only way you stop yourself doing this is by focussing on your thoughts. You lose the present by thinking you should be doing something else. Or you think about what others will be doing and compare what you're doing with what others are doing – and because we live in a world where we feel we should always be doing, you then generate disharmony, and forget that you're actually quite happy being yourself, with yourself, in this moment right now.

Let others 'do'. *You* can just 'be'.

💜 Live now, for you, with you.

Doodle, Scribble, Create!

I'd like you to experience a period of just 'being in the present' with no pressure, no specific thoughts, nowhere to be, nothing to do. You might need to make an appointment with yourself for this. It can be outside in nature, it can be in a library, a coffee shop, a park. It can be in your own living room with your pet on your lap. Wherever it is, aim to just be in the moment, with no judgement of yourself or of anyone or anything else. Try for at least half an hour. You're aiming to just 'be' with yourself and your thoughts, focusing on nothing in particular at all.

Doodle, scribble, create your experience of this, including how you're going to become a more natural and willing participant, and how you're going to factor more 'just be' time into your life.

You Can Live Spiritually

As I discussed in Part One, living spiritually means being true to yourself, believing in yourself, having confidence in your inner-most feelings, and living with love, compassion, care, appreciation, and acceptance. Spirituality is your beauty, your joy, your kindness, your laughter, your song. It is what we, as a species, were born with. Spirituality is our essence. It is our source. It is who and what we are. Over time, our societies have encouraged full use of ego-brain and discouraged or dismissed those who attempt to live compassionately and through their hearts.

If you are shining your light, then by default you are living spiritually. You are living love and dealing constructively and proactively with the messages coming to you through the fear.

Living spiritually means honouring *you*.

You Can Feel

I'm going to talk a bit about feelings here, separate to the rest of the senses, because I'm here to help you to pay attention to how you feel and to generate good, or at least better, feelings. I want you to feel free, well, healthy, happy, and full of joy. I want you to feel the freedom of letting go of – detaching from – the confines and burden of expectation. I want you to experience the feeling of living true to your heart. Everything I do is designed to inspire and encourage you to feel love, like, and contentment with yourself.

We're brought up that we're too fat, too thin, too tall, too short, too this, too that ... too imperfect altogether. Actually, all of that is unimportant. It is nobody's business, and it is completely secondary to who we are inside, where our light shines and our heart really speaks. Who we are inside is *not* encouraged. Not only is it not encouraged, it's crushed out of us. There's a lot to be said for living with and around people who encourage us, who commend us, and who accept us and love us for who and what we are, who give us hugs and assure us that they appreciate us just the way we are. There's even more to be said for being able to do this to ourselves.

It can be very difficult to actually stop and define how you're feeling. I often ask people what three things they're feeling 'right now', and it's quite interesting how difficult it is for some to answer and how uncomfortable others feel simply being asked the question. Children find it the most difficult, usually replying they 'don't know', turning away, getting embarrassed, and hoping I'll go away.

Answer that question yourself, right now. What three things are you feeling right now?

_____

_____

_____

If any of the answers are on the negative side, or revolve around 'bad' feelings, think about why you're feeling those feelings. Only then can you turn them around or improve them.

Most of us weren't and aren't taught about 'feelings' at school. We're not taught properly how to care about our inner selves and our constitutions.

> I understand now that I'm not a mess but a deeply feeling person in a messy world. I explain that now, when someone asks me why I cry so often, I say 'For the same reason I laugh so often – because I'm paying attention.'[33]
> Glennon Doyle Melton

In fact, on the whole, we're not brought up to *feel* at all. For most of my lifetime, feelings have been mocked or ignored as being something you talk about only while lying on a psychiatrist's couch. If you 'feel', then you're too sensitive, too precious, too soft. In the eyes of others who live through their egos, we who 'feel' become lesser beings.

Think for a minute about what's acceptable – what's the 'norm' – in our society. Let's take the media splattering people's private business all over its pages, manipulating the events and situations in people's lives. A world of individuals voluntarily picks up that printed media, reads it, judges its content, chats about it to others, and ultimately makes it acceptable to put someone's life through the wringer without a second thought about how these people might actually feel.

Imagine if that was being done to you. Or if that person was someone you love. How would you feel?

We have been fed so much fear that we've become numb to so much. We don't even stop for a minute to think about the innocent, undeserving, invaded person and their life and family. Or if we do, we're so enveloped in the arms of expectation and our own self-serving validity that we fail to speak up in support of that person. Our society, our governments, and many of our peers put money, greed, and 'self' first each and every time, and sadly, frighteningly, that's our normal. Even just writing this section and thinking about what we do to each other gives me the shivers.

Yet, having said all that, I believe that, as long as our establishment quietly deems that we all feel *fear*, then that's okay, their world is safe. As long as we're all living with a degree of anger, stress, guilt, worry, embarrassment, nerves, doubt, dishonesty, greed, anxiety, depression, as long as we're all lacking confidence and self-esteem, then the wheel will continue to turn and our pharmaceutical industry, our supermarket monopolies, and our banks and conglomerates will continue to thrive because we'll all remain unwell, in debt, scared, and highly insured. And because we do all live the fear, we can easily and quickly recognise those feelings and emotions.

Now imagine how we'd have grown up feeling if we lived in a world in which we all encouraged and empowered each other, if we smiled at each other, believed in each other, helped and enabled each other, laughed more, congratulated each other, enjoyed what we did during our days, and trusted each other. Imagine if we all felt energised and well!

Of course, to a certain degree, we need to know the negative before we can appreciate the positive. But how amazing if the balance were to change!

Talking about how we feel can make us feel vulnerable, inadequate, disempowered, out of control, and useless. That's because our heads are feeding us what to feel, not our hearts. I'm not going to dig deeply into the conformist Western history that's manipulated the way we've become and how too many of us feel; I think by now you'll have got the gist of my views. Suffice to say that I encourage you wholeheartedly to consider your own views – and to *feel* from the inside.

♥ You are an empathetic being.

Feel what it feels like to feel. Think about what it feels like to feel. Slow down. See if you can identify which feelings are generated from your head, and which are generated from your heart, from deep inside you. Acknowledge the different feelings you feel. All your feelings, whether they're from your head or your heart, are messages. They are your guidance system. Your feelings are more important to you than all the external voices coming in your face from every other angle – and believe me, once you start listening, they'll be the loudest and the clearest as well.

Your fear-related emotions are all heavy emotions that should play a part in your life only as messengers. They're not feelings or emotions you should feel for long periods of time. They don't have a full-time place in your life, and you *can* do something to diminish those weighty emotions. Consider these heavy feelings as indications that something needs to be attended to or changed in your life. And more importantly, take steps to do something about them.

I still live with plenty of fear-related feelings and emotions. They are conditioned lifetime habits that pull me away from my guidance from within. My friend, a few days ago, asked me what I gain from beating myself up with a big stick. I thought for a minute and replied that I gain 'nothing' from beating myself up with a big stick. 'You must get something or you wouldn't do it,' she replied. And she was quite right. We are enacting lifetime habits, expectations, and conditionings before we realise we're doing so, and it takes effort to restore the heart-head balance. But gradually it gets easier and quicker to restore, and having the right circle of friends and networks helps too because then you have a group of people who will help guide you back to love and your heart.

Most often it's just your reaction to something that needs to be changed. But that reaction can lead to three hundred other beat-me-up thoughts, and that's where it gets complex and difficult to follow what's actually going on. Our heads process so quickly that it's almost impossible to keep up with everything that goes through our minds even just in a few seconds.

Look for things that make you feel good, make you feel love and loved, make you smile, laugh and feel joy and deeply content. These are the things you want to be able to store so you can bring them to mind quickly when you notice yourself starting to feel negative. My sister and I can laugh till our sides ache and we've got tears pouring down our faces about observations that would hardly muster up mild amusement in anybody else. While I don't claim to have that reaction when I *think* of these times, I do grin from ear to ear, and it helps me to move out of and away from the negative feeling that was about to take hold. It helps me to keep perspective and then address, if necessary, whatever it was that was about to annoy me. You'll often find that you've moved on from whatever it was, and that it doesn't need any further attention because you realise it was nothing anyway.

This is also where magical photos in your phone can be good. And just this morning I was stopped in my tracks by the magic of two huge flocks of geese migrating in the calm early-morning autumn sky. The awesomeness of the natural world at work is indescribably grounding and can help very much in regaining perspective if you allow yourself to acknowledge it, connect with it, be with it, breathe into it. The demonstration of true teamwork amongst the geese was both striking and humbling, each bird taking a turn at the front, leading the way, easing the flight path for the others. Any goose that dropped back would be met by others who would help draw it back in. No goose was ignored or left alone. The birds communicated with ease; in fact, their chattering surrounded me like a warm blanket in the still, morning air. The whole experience was resounding and breathtaking, and the feeling I had as I observed those geese has stayed with me all day. You *can* consciously help the wonder of life to stay with you throughout the less than wondrous moments of your day. And by doing so, you find you have more and more – and more – to give thanks for each and every day.

And I've got to say it again – breathing and meditation. Take your focus away from whatever it is that's about to take hold of your mind, before it takes hold. Breathing is a winner.

You know what other kinds of things make you smile and help to cheer you up or bring you back to balance when you start to feel down. Whether it's memories, people around you, books, notes, words, keepsakes, or crystals. It might even be disappearing off to a place you know helps you. It might be a little happy notepad that you can flick through on which you've written a happy word, or a doodle, or a creation on each page!

Whatever works for you, make a collection and use it to your benefit.

> We are a lonely people scared of each other, of any difference,
> and rather than celebrating the abundance of diversity we fight
> wars because of it.[34]
> Rachel Corby

Doodle, Scribble, Create!

*Doodle, scribble, create a day in the life of feel good,
loving, loved and lovable, smiling, joyous you.*

*Consider what behaviours and conscious thoughts you'll
need to adjust to start creating and living as this person,
and then create and live as this person without delay.*

*Remember, you're on the adventure to let your light shine. Living the
feel-good, loving, patient, understanding you might feel like acting at
first. It might even feel fraudulent, but that's only because you've been
living with the conditions, expectations, and the resulting 'baggage' of
your upbringing for so long. This is you! It's time to set yourself free!*

Doodle, Scribble, Create!

Doodle, scribble, create the word joy on your page.

*Spend as long as it takes to create around the word
all the things in your life that bring you joy.*

*Keep adding to your joy, and use this happy page to remind
you of your bliss when you feel a fear-based moment coming on.
It would be very powerful to create your own little book of joy,
with one of your very own joys per page. Carry it around with
you everywhere and keep it within easy-reminder reach.*

Time With You

How much time do you spend alone? I won't presume to know the answer, but maybe you could spend more?

Our Western environment has encouraged full-time togetherness with a significant lack of privacy or time to catch up with ourselves. The more we are with or surrounded by others, the less likely we ever are to engage with or know our true selves.

Between that and the conditioning of our upbringings and our conformity to the expectations around us, it's no wonder that many of us actually avoid spending time alone with ourselves, away from our external environment. We don't know ourselves, and because we're a world of 'do-ers', we're not sure how to spend time just with ourselves, on our own, being with and getting to know *us*.

You really do need time alone. I try to avoid suggesting to people what they need to do, as I don't like being told what I need to do. It's your choice. You have your free will; it's your life. But I feel strongly that, if every member of humanity is to thrive instead of simply existing, which is what we're doing now, we all need regular time away from each other. Only then will we stop measuring ourselves up against and trying to keep up with each other. And we need to be more comfortable with that time away and more accepting of the need for it in each other.

It's not selfish to look after yourself; neither should you feel guilty about looking after yourself. You deserve time for yourself, and you *can* be strong and push back on people who suggest you don't need it – including yourself! Admit to yourself that you'd love time alone. And look at the people you're spending time with. Until you do, you probably don't realise just to what extent you allow the pressures and expectations of people around you to rule your life.

People can be draining, and life can be draining – unless you assert your power and give yourself the time and space you need and deserve. Your light will only ever continue to flicker the more time you spend with people, especially if they're people that don't serve you; it will burn brightly if you spend a bit of time on your own. And remember, the television, the radio and other media are people and life; computer games are virtual people and life. So when I say you need time alone, I mean you need time alone not watching or listening to, or reading, or playing with, anything highly stimulating that feeds you fear, condemnation, and high-energy stressors.

Find yourself a haven.

♥ You need *you*.

Spending time alone allows you to become more aware of yourself and who and what you are to yourself and to others. It helps to ground you; it helps you to regain perspective, and even find new perspective. It helps you to connect right back into who you really are, to balance your energy, and to reclaim your life. Being away from others gives you a chance to consider your emotions and your feelings, and to dig deeper into realising where some of your messages are coming from. By being alone you can recognise the sound and feeling of your heart's guidance without external distractions and expectations.

When you're alone, you can sit, you can be, you can breathe, you can create, you can process, you can listen, you can reflect. You can do whatever *you* want with no judgement, influence, pressure, argument, or explanation. The list of benefits time alone gives you is endless.

I'm not going to talk and talk about it. It's just something I strongly suggest you do, and regularly: make time for getting to know *you* and having *you* in your life.

♥ Get to know *you*.

Doodle, Scribble, Create!

I appreciate that you've already made time for you in your commitment to working through this book. But what happens once you've reached the end? Perhaps you could continue your commitment but replace your Live Your Sunshine – Be Your Light time with getting to know you better.

Doodle, scribble, create how you are going to make more time for yourself in your life. Start somewhere. If you currently have no time, doodle how you're going to create some. Even if you're a single mum, even if you're the dad of a family of four with a full-time job, no matter what your roles and responsibilities are in life, make this one of them. Being you with you. It will help you play all your roles more calmly and less stressfully.

If you currently enjoy some time alone but you know that deep down you need more, then doodle how you're going to create more.

Back to Your Senses

As you open up, you become more ready and able to pay attention to your feelings, tune into your senses, and receive the messages that are coming to you from inside and from your external energy and support system. Up till now, we've discounted your external world as having little good to offer, but that's because, collectively, we're stuck on what others in society have to say.

When we get back to nature and ground ourselves more, that external world is our world. That external world is the world we came from and the world that we're deeply a part of. That is the world to which we're connected: it is our home, our safe place, our anchor, and our joy.

That external world speaks to you in quite a different language from the external world you've been listening to and allowing to have so much control over your life up till now.

That beautiful world is what the bodies and egos in our lost world of humans are destroying, and it breaks my heart to write that line. We care less and less about our beautiful natural world, and we care less and less about each other as we all try to live in it, or even camp in it for a night or two. Our respect for each other and our magical environment has all but gurgled its last gurgle down the drain. What a sad, disappointing world to be living in.

Yet like attracts like. If we can all power together and help each other and respect each other and give to and for each other – like those dozens of migrating geese – we will create more and more pockets of goodness around the world, and those pockets will create more pockets, and soon our pockets will join and create huge sacks. And the sacks will join and create ... well, remember, the whole is worth more than the sum of its parts.

Your senses will help you love and appreciate the value that a beautiful world can have on the creation of you living your truth and shining your light. Our cities and our selves bog us down and we've lost – or a little more optimistically, we've simply forgotten – our understanding that the earth beneath our feet matters to our well-being. We are life according to nature, and we've allowed our relationship with our natural heritage to be obliterated by comforts, material objects, technology, ease, and convenience. When last did you rejoice to feel the wind blowing through your hair? When last did you open your arms, mouth, and eyes and lift your face up to catch the rain? When last did you stop and smell, feel, taste, breathe in, and listen to the atmosphere around you? When last did you stick your face in the long grass and inhale the smell of the earth, the soil beneath your feet?

> If we want greater physical and emotional well-being, we can
> use sounds, feelings, sights, tastes, and smells to balance and heal
> our selves.[35]
> Deepak Chopra, MD

We're caught up in a quagmire of thick, suffocating, toxic fog, and freedom and truth have eluded most of us for all of our lives.

But have they really? Could it be that we've just allowed them to pass us by because we've been focussing on the wrong things and ignoring what's around us at the cost of being told what is really 'right' or 'true' or 'appropriate'? Is it more to do with the fact that we've been led one way and forgotten that we can choose to go another way, or even another way, or another way? Have we forgotten that we can change our minds about what way we go? Are freedom and truth still there, waiting patiently around the corner for us to take advantage of as we haul our way out of the density, intensity, and crowdedness and remind ourselves of our senses and, more so, how to use them?

When you use your senses, you are in a better position to allow. You see, feel, hear, smell, taste; you pay attention, and sometimes you just finally settle down into the present and allow yourself to 'be'.

In this section, I'm going to go briefly through each of these senses and see what more we can do, that we have not already discussed, to unlock them and revitalise them.

Our senses can be subtle, but they can also be powerful and vital. Living our lives in and amongst the pollution of our societies, we miss the sounds of nature and the true tastes of good, wholesome foods. We don't listen to each other, and to add insult to injury, we also speak over each other *while* we're not listening.

We pay attention to things that don't serve us, and we don't pay attention to the things that will help us through our lives. We smell exhaust fumes, garbage, and toxicity instead of the bark of the rustic old birch tree, instead of the fresh air and the wild flowers.

We have been desensitised. Our senses have been flattened and suffocated.

But we *can* bring them alive again! We can choose to change some behaviours that will bring back vitality, beauty, and joy to our senses.

> ♥ Find freedom and truth through your senses. Your senses are your power.

Feeling, sensing, and allowing link us to the state of being open in the same way that intending does. You need to be open to be able to tune in to your feelings, pay attention to your senses, and receive the messages that are out there for you. You also need to be open to be able to appreciate the bliss and contentment in just being, which is what will help you receive your intentions.

Sensing is about tuning in – listening. And I don't always mean listening as in 'hearing'; I mean listening as in paying attention, getting a feel for what you're feeling or a sense of what you're sensing. It means *noticing* so that you see, hear, feel, and sense what's coming at you, what's out there for you. It's that sixth sense – that third-eye chakra, your centre for intuition, insight and imagination. Along with your intending and visualising, sensing helps to give you a feel for what the day's going to bring, what the outcome here is going to be, what's going to happen there, what direction to go in. Allow yourself to be receptive to everything that is around you and not only by listening to your mind. Ask for messages and be alert to signs.

Pay Attention

Remember how, when I resigned my job, I received my 'liberated' and 'believe' messages? Well, that's what I'm talking about here. There are messages that come to you through your senses and openness every day once you pay attention and allow yourself to receive.

The other day I was doing some yoga before I got myself going for the day. I was in a posture that reminded me of one of the yoga teachers I used to practise with when I lived in Australia. The thought led me to think of a lady who used to attend that class who had ancestral links to the area I'm from in Scotland. I thought very briefly of that lady with no force, no pressure; I just allowed the thought to come and go. I'd last been in touch with her three years ago, and I hoped she was doing well. About an hour later, I logged onto my computer to find that she had sent me an e-mail earlier that morning!

These sorts of things happen frequently when you're open and prepared to allow and receive. Here's another story: A very good friend of mine spent the night with her mum in a hotel the night before the second anniversary of my friend's brother's passing. It was to be a very personal and special evening for my friend and her mum, thinking about and celebrating Mark's life. The next day my friend's mum was going to fly out to America to spend time with Mark's wife and children. My friend loves Tunnock's Teacakes, and this is a well-known fact. So when she sent me a picture of the billboard that was sitting directly outside her airport hotel window – advertising you know what – we knew that it was her brother's way of saying 'hi' to his sister and his mum, and telling them he was okay and that they were to be okay.

Watch for – pay attention to – signs and messages that are there for you. They're not coincidences. They are synchronistic messages for you, guiding you and reassuring you on your adventure. And for the cynics and disbelievers, let's face it, even if this *was* a coincidence, isn't it powerful, perfect, comforting, and hilarious? We all laughed and laughed, and laughter is absolutely the best medicine. Synchronicity offers us positive experiences and messages, so try to open up to the positive. Whatever it was – and it was Mark – it was *right*.

Communications may not necessarily come to you as big messages, but they are reminders and confirmation that you're in tune and on track. Embrace occasions like these – large and small. They do matter, and they keep you on the right path and confirm that you're doing okay.

♥ Aim for the flow and then go with it.

If you discount events like these with cynicism, doubt, and negativity, you'll keep a part of you closed to opportunities, messages, and guidance that comes from your heart. If you can just open and accept, you'll go a long way. And when it comes down to it, what have you got to lose? What is there to gain from disbelieving, scorning, and doubting? Nothing! Nothing at all other than maintaining a level of closure and fear in your life for no good reason.

See and Look At

Look around you. Observe without judgement. Take in. Watch. Look at images and pictures of things that make you smile. Give your eyes a visual feast instead of continually looking at things you'd rather not see. Make your eyes happy, and bring things to their attention that make you smile and feel good inside. Here's an example: I've been away writing this week, but to have positive energy around me, I put a little plant with white flowers on my desk. I added some of my crystals and a couple of books that make me happy, and I made sure my notebooks and coloured pens and colourful spotty pencil case were nearby. Next to me are my heart chakra mouse pad and Steven D Farmer's Earth Magic oracle cards. I also have candles with various aromas around me and my dog for unconditional love, company, and hugs (and licks).

As I look up from my page and contemplate my flow and where I'm going next, I see one or more of these objects. And yes, they are objects. But I have selected them consciously, with purpose, as things that bring me joy. They are my 'medicine bag'. When I look up, I see happiness and healing, and I can continue in my stream of writing without being rudely interrupted by something 'unhappy' that takes away my momentum. I do also look up to see blue sky out one window and a mixture of different types of clouds moving slowly across the sky out the other. I see green grass in between my medicine bag items and the sky. I see the early autumn leaves on the trees. I see life and steadiness and sureness; I see support and reassurance. Everything's just right and doing what it does. In the bigger scheme of things, it doesn't matter if I finish this page today or tomorrow, as what I see reminds me that life and what's going on in our universe are so much bigger than I am, or the trains that fly past, or the cars that drive past, or the neighbours I have around me. We are small.

Explore the sights around you. Value your sight. Delight in the colours, the hues, the ever-changing shades of life around you. Stop. Look closely. Look up, look down, look all around. Examine, watch, observe, and ravage what brings your eyes joy. And find more of whatever brings your eyes joy.

Remember that bigger picture. Be conscious about what you choose to see and what you look at. Make it all nice. And as you get better at looking inside and following your internal guidance system, you'll receive *in*sight – inner sight – as well as outer sight.

♥ Look at the beauty of your bigger picture.

Listen and Hear

Sounds work the same as visuals. Be choosy about what you consciously allow yourself to listen to – to *hear*. If it doesn't work for you, think about why that is, and take steps to do something about it. If it's somebody who turns on the negativity or who grates on you when you hear them, then deal with that so it doesn't have the effect it has on you.

Listen to yourself as you converse with others. Do you actually listen? Do you allow other people the value of your listening skills, the respect of your attention? They are telling you things for a reason, because they think highly enough of you to want to share something with you. Or maybe they're answering questions you actually asked them. *Listen* to people when they're speaking to you. From a selfish perspective, it could actually add value to your life. But do it from a place of love. They've chosen to share their thoughts with you, so the least you can do is listen.

And then take time to consider and absorb what they've told you. We don't have to be talking all the time. You can't respond to someone effectively if you're too busy trying to work out how to reply because you're aware that soon they'll be finished and you can't respond with silence because silence is awkward.

Silence is golden! Not awkward! Accept that silence is golden, necessary, and required in your life, and not just during periods of communication either. If the silence feels awkward, tell the person you're just considering what they said, and giving the message the attention it deserves. Sometimes you might need to take a message away and think about it in your own space, without the speaker's energy around you. And that's okay! Spending the time working out how to reply means your ego has taken over and your head is too busy processing ways not to feel self-conscious with silence. Don't be ego centred; be heart centred. Listen with your heart and focus on what the other person is telling you.

The world doesn't revolve around talking, and because so much of the time what's being said isn't being listened to properly anyway, because we're too busy being distracted or working out our response (the importance of which is, in our minds, immediacy rather than quality), what we say to each other ends up being superficial, messy, and often just words for the sake of words.

Converse quietly, soundly, and with thought. Listen quietly, soundly, and with consideration and respect. Enjoy the silence and increase the quality of your conversation.

♥ Respect the other person; listen to what they are telling you.

But that's not just what listening and hearing are about!

There are birds around you. There are trees, insects, and other life forms around you. In towns and cities, the extent of our domestication is such that we either don't hear these sounds, or we are irritated by them. Closer to country areas, we hear much more than the limited beautiful and natural sounds we've removed from our lives. We hear true nature. For me, there's nothing more beautiful and calming than the sound of very light rain on a still Scottish loch. When everything else is silent, that must be one of the most soothing, peaceful sounds my ears have ever been blessed to hear. I can just be with that experience for a long time.

Sounds should bring us joy, and joy comes in so many different guises: The sound of a voice you love. The sound of a fire crackling. The sound of your favourite song. The sound of a whisper. The sound of nothing. At the moment I'm enjoying hearing the sound of the wind in the early autumn trees, and my dog in some level of ecstasy as he wriggles around on his back in the sunshine on the lush green grass.

💜 Hear the pure sounds of life.

I've debated over whether to talk about music and instrumental sound here or under 'feel'. It is, essentially, sound, but music – indeed all sound – is vibration. You *feel* music and sound just as much, if not more, than you hear it or listen to it. It really doesn't matter where the topic sits though, especially in a book where we're focussing on your feelings anyway. Hear it first and foremost and then focus on how it makes you feel.

I found I avoided music for a long time. It would fill me with sentiment or memories or make me think of things or people, or it would grate on me, interrupt me, scream at me, or just not be the right thing to be listening to for what I was doing or looking for at the time.

Then I got a bit more curious and started to look for music that would make me feel good. And didn't I come alive! Music, including, I realised, a lot of percussion and instrumental sounds that make me feel good – no, not good, amazing! – comes in various forms.

Music and instrumental sound should be something very personal to you; it should uplift *you*, relax *you*, energise *you*, wash over you and through you like it was inside *you*, and beat through your blood vessels as if it *is you!*

♥ Love what moves *you.*

Allow yourself to become fully absorbed in music and instrumental sounds. I was stunned at the incredible impact the slow drumbeat of a hand-held drum had on me during a shamanic journey. I was with a small group, lying outside on the grass. The guide was taking us on the journey while slowly beating the drum. When the guide came closer to me, I *felt* that drum in a way I can't quite describe. I had never felt a drum like that before. It captured my heart, it pumped my heart, and it gently beat through me even as it continued on past me. I wanted to burst! I wanted to call it back! That beat alone overpowered anything visual I was doing at that point in time. It was highly invigorating!

The drum is often used in shamanic journeys and in meditation to help create a level of grounding back to our roots, and calm. A state of calm is conducive to slightly shifting your state of consciousness away from everyday thoughts to the more subtle, blissful, and beautiful realms I mentioned in the meditation section. The drum in this case drew me completely away from anything the guide was saying, and I just lavished in the feel of the vibration, willing it to come back towards me and eat me up.

On that same retreat – the vision quest I mentioned earlier – I grew so connected to my environment that I could hear a dry leaf rustling in the lightest breath of wind, then falling onto several other dry leaves. I got a fright the first time it happened as it was close and sounded like something much bigger than it was. Similarly, other sounds of leaves, insects, and the breeze were amplified as my hearing became highly sensitive.

As you get better at listening to *you* and following your internal guidance system, you'll notice more of your internal messages, and you'll begin to keep those constant external messages at bay.

I'm going to offer you two activities in relation to listening and hearing, each quite different from the other.

> ♥ Listen to and hear the beauty of your bigger picture. It's inside you, and it surrounds you.

Doodle, Scribble, Create!

Spend at least a day paying attention to your behaviour when someone is talking to you. Do you really listen? Do you interrupt? Do you let the other person finish before you start to talk? Do you respond without thought? Would you enjoy speaking with you, or trying to tell you something?

Doodle, scribble, create your observations and what you are going to do to become a better listener.

Doodle, Scribble, Create!

Go onto YouTube and search various types of music. Don't just go to what you know. In fact, don't go to what you know. Think up some words that open up a search – New Age, relaxation, up-beat, shamanic drumming, Inca wind pipes, energising, deep cleansing – anything. It's up to you, but use these curiosity juices you've caused to flow and see what you can find.

Try at least five different types of music and sounds and doodle, scribble, create below how each one makes you feel.

Taste and Smell

While these appear to be two separate senses, without our nose or our sense of smell, we wouldn't be able to taste more than three quarters of the foods we eat. Notice that you are already savouring dinner as the kitchen fills with the aroma of your cooking. Indeed, you often savour the aroma more than you do the actual food! Notice how, when you inhale that longed-for coffee, you can almost taste it in your mouth.

Notice when you breathe in deeply, you can taste and smell the wonder of the fresh air around you. Your senses love nature. They devour nature. Nature and your natural surroundings take you back to your senses in the truest form.

Yet, although we have several thousand taste buds on our tongues and several million neurons in our noses, our senses of taste and smell have also been desensitised by our polluted environment and the genetically modified, processed, artificially flavoured, pesticide-sprayed foods that we eat. All too often we no longer notice or pay attention to many of the smells around us: the wood-burning fire in the winter, today's bread baking in the bakery, the freshly cut grass, the buttercups in our local park. Our noses have become numbed by chemicals, toxins, gases, and other pollutants, and our brains don't alert us to the vibrancy of the aromas around us.

We eat with our eyes. We no longer savour our food as an 'event'. We eat quickly, we eat bland, we eat processed, and we eat convenience. Eat a meal blindfold and see what you experience. Immediately your taste buds are enhanced. Savour what you're eating. Take time with it and enjoy the sensations of the different flavours, the different textures, the different tastes. Feel the way your food is processed around your mouth as part of your digestion.

💜 Savour food as an event.

We can enjoy using only our taste and our smell. Remove words, eyes, and touch, and eating becomes a whole new sense experience we've never realised. We can often perform better while doing other things too when we close our eyes. I often close my eyes when I'm listening intently to something. It helps me to zone out the distractions and focus purely on what I'm hearing. When we eat with our eyes, we're expecting things to taste a certain way, and so they do, even when they're actually a little 'light on' in the flavour department. We've come to accept this because we're too busy looking or focusing elsewhere, or chatting. We allow our other senses to overpower our true enjoyment of our food. We don't look for or want – or even know about – the six flavours believed to bring us satisfaction and optimal nutrition: salty, sweet, sour, astringent, pungent, bitter. Or even just the most basic four: salty, sweet, sour, bitter. Perhaps when we have five or six of these tastes we feel at our most satisfied, but I suspect we will have achieved that satisfaction mostly by accident. We have lost our connection with food just as we have with our environment.

If you've ever fasted for any length of time, you'll know your taste buds catch on fire when you return to good, wholesome, simple foods and meals. Wow! Fasting, in fact, is another thing that's becoming scientifically proven as incredibly effective for our overall health and well-being – physically, mentally, emotionally, and spiritually. Food suppresses our emotions so it makes sense that periods of fasting help to cleanse, balance, and nurture our whole selves. Not to mention giving us space where we don't have to think about food, plan food, buy food. That, alone, is incredibly freeing.

Food is our grace, our lifeline, our nourishment. Yet fasting, too, is our grace, our lifeline, our nourishment. Four days fasting in the wild for me was invigorating, calming, cleansing, and deeply satisfying.

Again, to realise what your nose is missing, spend some time out in true nature. Wild flowers and the startlingly strong smells of nature waft around you, making their way up your nose and into your being.

In the town and city, stop and inhale the smell of whatever nature offers on whatever day or month of the year it is – the deep rose of late October, the powerful first hyacinth or the jasmine vines of the spring, the beautiful trailing sweet peas of the summer, the straw bales and earthy farm smells of the autumn. Get into parks and gardens as much as you can when it's difficult to step into the countryside.

Smells connect us to so much of life. They can bring back memories, they can elicit strong feelings and emotions, and they can strike us profoundly, deep down inside totally out of the blue. It can be very useful to consciously connect certain smells and aromas of your choosing to good feelings, joyful experiences, happy thoughts, and smiling faces.

Essential oils are the pure natural oils of plants and are beauty to your nose. You can do a lot with essential oils. You can burn them, dilute them with a carrier oil and apply them to your skin, bathe in them, put a few drops on a tissue or on your pillow. You'll be drawn to certain smells, and certain smells can help your mood.

> When we smell something, we are actually absorbing some of its molecules, making aromatherapy a form of natural medicine.[36]
>
> Deepak Chopra MD

You Can Connect With Nature

Without the elements we wouldn't be alive. For starters, over half of our bodies are water.

Yet on the whole, we treat nature and the magical world around us with contempt or at best acceptance. We don't value it; neither do we appreciate it. The natural world around us is where we came from. It's our roots. The grounding and rightness we can feel when we to connect back with the quietness of our natural world is powerful, empowering, and humbling all at the same time. It can also feel humiliating at times to think that we're a part of the humanity that's destroying it. Yet it is also reassuring and a reminder of what is really important – far more important than *anything* else in our lives because without it – without air, water, fire, and earth, without ether and light, without sun and moon – we wouldn't be here.

If the gravity from the moon causes the tides, and we're made up of more than fifty percent water, then shouldn't it hold true that we are directly affected at times by the draw of the moon?

Rachel Corby, author of *Rewild Yourself: Becoming Nature*, suggests that our conditioning to our society as well as our disconnection from nature starts as soon as we're born.

> Rather than allowing the baby to follow its natural cycle of when it needs nourishment, sleep, nurture and actually connect with its own body's needs, the infant is required to fit into someone else's schedule. Baby is fed and put to sleep by the hands of the clock, a sure interpretation of animals (human animals) as machines, with no room for our individual differences, no acceptance of the fact that some of us will grow to be huge while others will always be petite with related differences in appetite. This is most people's first experience of a disconnect from Gaia.

> If fed by routine, not demand, when you ask for your most basic need to be met – food – there is no response. What a lonely path to commence this life journey upon. It is a very young age to be introduced to the myth that we are detached from the world, and our actions (asking for food) have no direct relation to what happens in our world (being fed). Unfortunately the preconception that our actions remain separate from what happens in the world around us, for many of us, was one of the first things we learned.

> We are taught such lonely lessons so early on. We also find that things we do not need in the moment (sleep and food) are presented to us anyway, with no connection to the timing of

our needs. We quickly learn to take it while we can; because if we don't, and then ask for it later, we will just go hungry, sleepless and ignored, possibly even chided. The impact of these early lessons on our belief systems is far reaching. As we go through life so many of us just take everything in excess when it is presented regardless of potential consequences, whether it is cake, coffee or cocaine – until at some point something breaks. We don't hear our bodies say no, perhaps we don't even know how to hear them, how to listen, as their pleas and cries have been ignored for so long.[37]

Rachel Corby

We *need* our natural world. It's not just the sun, the moon, and the elements that affect us; the movements of some of the planets around space are also known to have a direct effect on us down here. Remember, we're all energy living in an energy universe, so of course other things are going to affect us. And it's time we allow ourselves to accept that we are a part of this and that it's time to connect back to our natural world. We need space, time out, silence, and stillness to thrive. It's our healing. Look around you. Feel inside you. Collectively, we're not thriving; we're merely existing. We want to feel grounded, we want much more of the feeling that we're going to burst with joy, sing with thanks, and shout from the rooftops that we love being alive.

When I was talking about our senses in the last section, I mentioned that many of us who live in cities are more often irritated by insects and birds than we are pleased. We go out our way to kill, to swat, to stand on living things that are small enough to be removed from our existence because, from our stance of superiority, they are annoying us or they might 'do something' to us.

We wouldn't be where we are now, in the state we're in now, if we grounded ourselves in our roots regularly and remembered to keep things in perspective. This world was given to us as a gift, yet it has become alien. Nature is ours to live with and to be part of while we experience our time on earth. It's not ours to abuse or to destroy for our own gain. What we do to nature we do to ourselves. What humans do to our earth, we do to our race – the race of humankind – because we are all one. What humans do through their own fear – their greed, their dishonesty, their arrogance – they do to their own.

Maybe our lives would be easier and nicer if we considered ourselves as guides and leaders instead of parents – guides and leaders in the true essence of the words. That would make us similar to the indigenous elders in their roles. Perhaps if we had guides and leaders instead of teachers and ministers or priests, we would all feel a little more connected to and accepted by each other. True guides and leaders have respect for those they're guiding and leading. True guides and leaders know and accept that we are all equal and that not only can they impart their expertise to their 'guidees', they can learn from their guidees. Parents, teachers, and ministers often view themselves not just in positions of authority, but as people of authority, superior to their children, their students, and their followers.

True guides and leaders give guidance and receive guidance. None of us knows all there is to know.

Disconnect from your society world and connect back to your natural world. Ground yourself in nature. Feel it and just 'be' it. This is where you'll find your truth. If you really want to shine your light and find peace within you *need* nature and its natural sounds and stillness.

> Geologists describing the evolution of our planet have subdivided the history of the Earth into 'chapters' called Ages or Epochs. From the end of the last 'ice age,' about 11,700 years ago until recently, the planet has been in what geologists call the *Holocene Age*. However, we have just entered a new geological age, the *Anthropocene*. This period is defined as the era when human activity became the dominant influence in shaping Earth system processes, such as climate and the environment.[38]
>
> Dr Bruce Lipton

Doodle, Scribble, Create!

Set aside at least one hour for yourself, preferably more, and go to a place in nature, making sure it's a place where you won't be disturbed or interrupted. Either sit or walk, or both, but spend this hour observing, absorbing, and feeling the natural world around you. Just be in the present and love it for everything it is.

Use all your senses and devour the life. Watch busy insects and birds, smell the air, connect to the sky, follow the clouds, smell the season, take in the beauty and strength of that magical cycle that we so easily forget we are a part of. Inhale the flowers, the natural sights, and the energy.

Doodle, scribble, create your experience.

You Can Move

No, I'm not here to tell you to go to the gym, or do half an hour of exercise every day, or get a six-pack so you can match up to the person whose body has been Photoshopped and featured on the cover of the latest fitness magazine. I'm not here with any of the mundane tiresome orders that come your way from various other sources. I'm here to suggest that you *move*, that you *can* move, and that you should do so in whatever way feels right to you.

In hindsight, just about every section under 'You Can' could have sat under 'You Can Open Up' because, if you can open up, you can do every other thing I've talked about. That would be one big chapter!

But I said that about being grateful too. This whole book could have been written under 'Being Grateful'.

I was thinking the same thing as I was writing about getting back to nature. Getting back to nature provides you with the space you need to open up, to realise your appreciation, to breathe deeply, and to just be – with yourself. Everything I've talked about could have come out of living with nature.

Just as, in our world and our universe, everything is connected, every part of this book is connected to the next, and while there's a structure, every part enhances every other part.

But, anyway, my point is that, if you've opened yourself up to trying new things, if you've already become curious and stepped outside your comfort zone, then you'll be ready to take what comes when I talk about moving.

Wriggle and shake, stretch and crumple, kick and swipe, walk and run, jump and hop – that's all there is to this one. You can dance, march, bend, swivel, clomp, sway. You can do whatever you like! Moving is invigorating, energising, and cleansing. It's restful, relaxing, and calming. So for those reasons, I'd like to suggest you get it into your day. Get up and move. Find your invigorating music and go for broke.

♥ Move your body to free your energy.

Although I'm talking about moving more so than stretching and balancing at this point, if you do nothing at all in your day, then a bit of swaying and a bit of yoga would be a good start. Yoga helps you to stretch, and swaying and moving around help you get used to postural movements and simply moving your body in ways it feels it needs to be moved.

At the very least, I do some yoga and stretches in the first hour after I get up in the morning. I don't do them as a routine, and I don't do them strictly, but I do *do* them. I do them in my own time, and I do whichever stretches and postures feel like the ones I need on the day. You don't need to follow any routine. The only thing I suggest is that, if you've never tried yoga, try it, even just a handful of times. Go to a class first, as the teacher will make sure you've got the postures correct so you don't do yourself any damage. If you love it, keep going; if you don't particularly love it, or if you find it difficult to get to, use it as an opportunity to learn some stretches that you can do at home.

I also learned recently about postural energetics, which I'm finding highly effective. Postural energetics is a part of a treatment called Kinetic Chain Release™. Stand on the same spot with your feet hip distance apart and move in whatever way your body takes you for, basically, as long as you like. The length of several songs, or ten or fifteen minutes would be good. I won't talk too much about this, as it's new to me; essentially, it helps to move and clear your energy.

And then there's Chakra Dancing, which is postural energetics times one hundred!

Do feel free to take your curiosity on another little adventure and find out more yourself.

Just before we move on from here, let's remember that a walk in nature can be part of your 'moving' exercises, and it also can:

- Connect you back to nature.
- Be your time out.
- Be your alone time.
- Be your 'be' time.
- Generate so much love – whether you're out with your dog, on your own, looking at wild flowers, smelling the fresh air and the atmosphere, lying on lush green grass looking at a blue sky, or enjoying winter sunshine and the crisp feeling of being alive.

Don't discount the benefits you can get from simply getting yourself away and taking your time out in nature. Nature is my saviour.

♥ Is nature your saviour?

Doodle, Scribble, Create!

*Use the amazing new sounds you invited into your new
life in the last section, and get up and move.*

*Use your sounds, your music, your instrumentals, your musicians,
your body. Sway, jump, shake, kick your legs, stretch, flow, wave your
arms. Give yourself the gift, allow yourself to receive the gift, enjoy
the gift of energising, empowering, free, and flowing movement.*

Spend at least twenty minutes doing this.

Doodle, scribble, create how it made you feel.

You Can Be True to You

THERE IS SOMETHING VERY MUCH BIGGER than you and much nicer and more trusted and loving than much of what's around you. Believe in it – it believes in you – and call it forth to work with you as you turn a bend or a welcome sharp corner in your life.

> Truth or reality is avoided when it is painful. We can revise our maps only when we have the discipline to overcome that pain. To have such discipline, we must be totally dedicated to the truth. That is to say that we must always hold truth, as best we can determine it, to be more important, more vital to our self-interest, than our comfort. Conversely, we must always consider our personal discomfort relatively unimportant and, indeed, even welcome it in the service of the search for truth. Mental health is an ongoing process of dedication to reality at all costs.[39]
>
> M. Scott Peck, MD

Don't surrender your chance of happiness, enjoyment, and peace within to others. As humans we have a tendency to mock things we don't know about or understand. That then excuses us from participating. It can also make life quite shallow for us because we're not allowing ourselves the opportunity to open up to new experiences, to learn, to try. We're scared we'll be laughed at, insulted, or misunderstood if we don't stick with everyone else's flow, that same 'ego-centred' flow we were brought up to go with, rather than the 'heart-centred' flow we were born to go with.

I was quite self-conscious when I started telling people I was going to a meditation group. Over a very brief period of time, however, my interest in meditation became a very natural part of my social life and with that came easy, confident communication about it. I got used to the fact that, if I'm telling my truth, with consideration and compassion – which is what you do and how you live when your heart chakra finds balance – as well as being open, honest, and speaking who I am, then the judgements remain with others to deal with in whatever way they choose.

At the same time, I had a habit of putting 'expected' judgements of others on myself. That was my ego talking. That was my ego telling me what to expect when it's got no right to do that. I had to find a way to stop doing that so that I could assertively and openly speak my truth without being self-conscious or expecting a particular response.

If someone can't accept that you're meditating – and I'm just using that as an example – or if somebody puts you down, or meditation down, or both (and they will), don't give in to them and don't justify or excuse yourself. Stand tall and strong, and remember that the issue – the fear – belongs to the other person. I've mentioned a few times that it's easier for people to knock that which they don't know or understand. That's what people do. Same as they might laugh if you wear something colourful and unique, or look a bit different. It's their way to deal with their fear of the unknown. In this life we're brought up to put down, judge, and criticise what we don't know or what we don't do, or wear, ourselves. How many times have I said that now?

If you speak your truth and somebody doesn't like it, if you've spoken genuinely, and if you've spoken in a way that's synchronistic with the conversation that's being had – normal, open, 'loving' conversation and sharing of information – then you can be comfortable with that. The other person must work with any reaction or overreaction. As you become more comfortable being *you*, you'll detach from the reactions of others.

It can be hard speaking your truth when you're surrounded by people you think won't and don't understand. Especially when you're only getting used to speaking it to yourself! Just take it easy and gradually. Give them one snippet of the new you at a time. They'll gradually get used to knowing a subtly different you. Many will accept and embrace that. Many will encourage your new interests, your new ideas, and some will even ask what you're reading now, or enquire as to your latest pursuits. Others might draw away from you – as might you from them. That's okay. Go forward on your adventure gently, patiently and from a place of love both for others and for yourself. What will be will be; don't stick to the past just because you know it. Venture forth as *you* and everything will fall into place for you along the way. Have faith and believe in *you* and the rest will work itself out.

💜 Take a deep breath and come from your heart.

Resolutions – New Year, New Month, New Day

The good old New Year's resolution has been the topic of many a bored groan and derisive laugh, but if you like an end and a beginning, if you like a little something tangible to work on, then the New Year's resolution definitely serves its purpose. I use New Year's resolutions every year. For this year, in line with my own personal and spiritual development, I committed to relinquish judging and being critical of others. It's quite incredible how often we do this in our lives without consciously thinking about it, and it's not a nice thing to do. In fact, it takes energy. It's consuming. I'm finding it much nicer just being, just getting on with my own business rather than finding fault with others.

That doesn't mean I've fallen in love with everybody. It means I don't spend time or energy or waste emotion on people I find challenging for one reason or another. I keep focussed on my own part and reason for being in that situation at that point in time rather than getting all tied up with what people are saying to me or how they are saying it or how they're looking at me or what they're blaming me for or how they're judging me. I'm working on accepting others for who and what they are, and if they've got anger or some other negative-related issues, I'm working on accepting them as who they are, just as I am who I am and expect them to allow me that freedom. If they have angry or negativity-related issues, those are their responsibility, not mine to take on and carry about. I figure if someone annoys me, then I need to look at what I can do to not be annoyed by that person.

♥ Let others get on with their business, and you get on with yours.

I'm not saying you need to make New Year's resolutions, but do consider whether the closure and opening of a period of time for you helps you to take on a small change. Maybe your birthday, maybe the beginning of a new month, maybe the beginning of the school year, maybe the start of the next quarter, or the new moon. Or you can begin something new with no structure or end or beginning. We're all different, and it would be great to know the different ways some of you work with the content of this book. It's all ideas, tips, and suggestions. We're all in this together.

Live your life with love and let others get on with their business. It makes for a much nicer adventure. I'm bursting to think of some of you really taking this on, taking the lead of your life, and I am *so* there with you. You can *so* do it. You're an amazing star – go shine!

♥ Make more 'I never want this to end' moments in your life.

Doodle, Scribble, Create!

Go back to the second-last activity in Part One in which you identified a fear-based emotion you were feeling. Consider now the steps you were taking to deal with that fear. Is it still rampant in your life? Or has something else taken its place? If the answer to either or both of these is yes, now consider everything you've worked through in Part Two and doodle, scribble, create a plan of action so that this fear message dissolves, enabling you to forgive and focus on loving feelings.

It's hard to change the habits of a lifetime, but you can change them with focus, effort, patience, belief, and commitment. Stick at it, beautiful. You're worth it!

Doodle, Scribble, Create!

Doodle, scribble, create five things you love about yourself.

*L*ive Your Sunshine,
Be Your Light

WELL, YOU FREE BIRD! YOU'VE MADE it! Congratulations.

Thank you for sticking with this all the way through. Your commitment, focus, and will to change your life *will* pay off. This is one small book in one huge world of ever-increasing information, evidence, research, change, and new findings. Stick with it all, keep in touch, and when you feel you're going off track, remember to breathe deeply, all the way down, and look for the love and guidance in whatever it is you're doing or going through.

In working through this book, you have put your truth before your comfort. Congratulations on everything you've achieved! The more pain and discomfort you've been through, the bigger the congratulations!

Your light is shining brighter again, and you are going to *love* living your sunshine. I hope you already are! I wish I could share all of your progress, but know inherently that I commend you. I encourage you to stay in the right direction on this new part of your adventure. By now you will know what that is. Speak your truth and live authentically and true to *you*.

You have put *so much* of yourself into getting to where you are now. You have put an enormous amount of energy, patience, and commitment into changing aspects of your self and your life. To close off, I was going to ask you to doodle, scribble, create the top three main life changing factors you've taken from your experience of working through this book and how you are applying them in your life to become new habits and beliefs. But then I thought, that's just confirming what you're already doing. Where's the challenge in that? That doesn't change a thing!

So, to close off, I'm going to ask you to doodle, scribble, create *one more thing* you're going to do in your life that you've been avoiding or hiding from. Make a resolution. Take *one more step* out of your comfort zone and consider how you're going to plant this *one more life-changing activity* into your life to become a new habit and belief.

❤ Remember, you are power, you are strength, you are beauty, you are love, you are light.

Doodle, Scribble, Create!

Doodle, scribble, create one more thing you're going to do in your life that you've been avoiding or hiding from. Take one more step out of your comfort zone and consider how you're going to plant this one more life-changing activity into your life to become a habit and belief.

Then take time to commend yourself on your achievements and progress. Go shine your light, earth angel! You are amazing!

*W*here to Now

IT TOOK ME TWO-AND-A-HALF MONTHS TO seriously work my way through Denise Linn's *Soul Coaching®* book. When I reached the end of it, I felt a little 'lost'. I'd been very conscious that I was approaching the end, and I felt a little melancholy as I worked through my last few exercises, as if I was preparing to leave a good and trusted friend. Denise's guidance had become a huge and a very powerful part of my life, as had her presence. I had stretched myself to horizons I'd never reached before. I'd been challenged – and had risen to the challenge – by thought-provoking questions and exercises.

Reaching the end of the course was amazing. It was exciting, it was daunting, and it was empowering. I was a little concerned. Would I manage to maintain the changes I'd been making? Would I return to old habits? Could I do it without the coach keeping me right?

But my biggest question was – what now? I was faced with a bit of an anti-climax. Where did I go next? I wanted stage two. I wanted the next bit. But I didn't know what that was, or where to look.

But it wasn't the end. It was another beginning – the start of me living as *me*.

Now that you've reached the end of this book, you might feel the same as I did. After such a huge and personal undertaking, you might feel similar emotions. And I want to say this to you: Trust yourself. Have faith in yourself. Believe in yourself. You are amazing. You are capable, you are able, and you are empowered. You have everything you need to continue your unique adventure with your newfound inner *you*.

Keep all your notes. Keep working on your conscious changes. Allow yourself plenty time to embed the new subtle changes that make you *you*. Make short- and long-term goals and resolutions. Give thanks every day for every single one of your successes, no matter how small. Rejoice in all of these successes. Remember to keep intending, visualising, feeling, and believing. Look for the love in everything that you do. Check back over your notes and keep giving yourself the space, the time, and the nature you deserve. You are coming into your own. *You* are coming back. Be gentle with yourself, be patient with yourself, and listen to – and heed – that friend inside.

Spend time with *you* so that the subtle new changes that make you *you* can settle, can really take root and establish themselves. Continue enriching, nurturing, and nourishing your new relationship with yourself. The next step will come from you simply being yourself, listening in the right places and paying attention to the messages. What's next for you will come at the right time, in the right form, and probably from the place you least expect it. All you need to do is focus on being *you* and being true to *you*. Take it easy. Allow yourself to flow. This is the beginning for you. Embrace everything that you are.

Please do share with me, speak to me. I'd love to hear about your successes, about where you're at, about your adventure and your achievements. It's an up-and-down, in-and-out, bumpy old adventure, but they're the best kind, and they're what you make them.

Go and shine! You *are* and you *can*.

> Follow your bliss and don't be afraid, and doors will open where
> you didn't know they were going to be.[40]
> Joseph Campbell

*T*hank You to My Guides

Esther and Jerry Hicks, authors of a series of books based on the teachings of a group of non-physical entities collectively called Abraham

Denise Linn: *Soul Coaching®: 28 Days to Discover Your Authentic Self*

Denise Linn and Meadow Linn: *Quest: A Guide for Creating Your Own Vision Quest*

Neale Donald Walsch: *Conversations with God: An Uncommon Dialogue*

Don Miguel Ruiz: *The Four Agreements: A Practical Guide to Personal Freedom* (A Toltec Wisdom Book)

Richard Carlson: *Stop Thinking Start Living: Discover Lifelong Happiness*

Bev Aisbett: *Letting IT Go: Attaining Awareness out of Adversity*

Dr Wayne Dyer, philosopher and self-help author

Doreen Virtue, founder of Angel Therapy

Gregg Braden, New Age author

Me and my inner shining light

The world around me

My most difficult experiences

Angry people and their baggage

Numerous other amazing people, diverse personalities, and everyday encounters that have touched my life in one form or another

*B*ooks on My Shelf Today

BOOKS HAVE COME AND GONE FROM my bookshelf over the years, most forwarded on to someone who hopefully got at least as much from them as I did. I've mentioned a handful throughout my book. The current residents on my bookshelf are, in no particular order:

- *When I Loved Myself Enough* by Kim McMillen with Alison McMillen
- *The Road Less Travelled* by M. Scott Peck, MD
- *Walking in Light: The Everyday Empowerment of a Shamanic Life* by Sandra Ingerman
- *Rewild Yourself: Becoming Nature* by Rachel Corby
- *The Magic Path of Intuition* by Florence Scovel Shinn
- *Angel Therapy: Healing Messages for Every Area of Your Life* by Doreen Virtue and the Angelic Realm
- *Soul Coaching®: 28 Days to Discover Your Authentic Self* by Denise Linn
- *Quest: A Guide for Creating Your Own Vision Quest* by Denise Linn and Meadow Linn
- *Phoenix Rising* by Mary Summer Rain
- *The Reason I Jump: One boy's voice from the silence of autism* by Naoki Higashida
- *Wild: An Elemental Journey* by Jay Griffiths
- *The Lady And The Generals: Aung San Suu Kyi And Burma's Struggle for Freedom* by Peter Popham

- *The Fifth Agreement: A Practical Guide to Self-Mastery* (A Toltec Wisdom Book) by Don Miguel Ruiz and Don Jose Ruiz with Janet Mills
- *The Act of Will* by Roberto Assagioli, MD
- *Journey To Creating Harmony Within* by Heather McCabe
- *Big Magic: Creative Living Beyond Fear* by Elizabeth Gilbert
- *Wild Mind: A Field Guide to the Human Psyche* by Bill Plotkin
- *Really Important Stuff My Dog Has Taught Me* by Cynthia L. Copeland
- I also have a book on quantum mechanics and a book on border collies

I am drawn to certain books, and when I'm drawn, I purchase. Sometimes I get what I need from them simply by having purchased them.

Quest: A Guide for Creating Your Own Vision Quest is an example. I was drawn to it as soon as I walked into the Crystal Shop in St Andrews one Saturday in April 2016. It was sitting on its own, on the bottom shelf of a display of various holistic and crystal gifts. I walked straight to it, bent down, and picked it up. Many of the exercises in Denise Linn's book, *Soul Coaching®*, had brought me a long way in my spiritual growth in a very short time, so I wasn't surprised to note that the book I was so drawn to was written by Denise Linn and Meadow Linn.

As I was wandering around the shop I glanced through the book and noticed it contained exercises. This excited me, as that's what I'd loved about Denise before. She made me think differently and higher – maybe 'bigger', wider, broader – about things than I ever had. She did for me what I'm trying to do for you in the chapter 'You *Can* Open Up'. I also noticed the book was about preparing for a vision quest. For a moment I paused and thought, *Hmm, I've never heard of a vision quest and I'm not going on one so should I get this book.* However, that moment passed, and my intuition remained in situ over my doubting head. (That's a good example of where I'd love you to get to – the point where you can tell, and acknowledge, which part of you is speaking, and keep it constructive but follow your inner guidance.) I knew that, vision quest or not, I would grow from this book and, along with a few other items that promised me well-being and calm, I bought the book.

♥ Go with your sixth sense. You don't have to have a reason.

That night I had a flick through the early pages before bed and my resident butterflies started fluttering. I liked what I was reading. What *was* this 'quest' that took readers away from humanity into nature and left them to their own devices for days? How incredibly exciting! My head was tired but my insides were wide awake and very alive, so I proceeded to Google 'Vision Quest Scotland'. Lo and behold, staring back at me was information on a vision quest taking place in Scotland, that year, in August 2016. I was jumping.

That's what listening to your intuition is about. On Saturday, 16 April 2016, I had been guided to that book having never heard of a vision quest before. And on Tuesday, 16 August 2016, I ventured out with five other vision questers from around Europe, for four days, to our very own little sanctuaries of alone-ness and bliss in the Scottish Highlands, with little more than a tarpaulin, a sleeping bag, the clothes we had on, and several litres of water.

I haven't read every single word in all of these books, but every single one of these books is a friend, a companion. These books support me when I feel doubt. Many of the authors of these books believe in me and what I'm doing. When I feel doubt, I go to my bookshelf and I listen to my guides. These are the people who inspire me to know and to remember that I *can*.

We all can.

Doodles, Scribbles, Creations!

Doodles, Scribbles, Creations!

Doodles, Scribbles, Creations!

Doodles, Scribbles, Creations!

Thanks ...

Thanks …

Thanks …

Thanks …

References

1   Gregg Braden, *The Spontaneous Healing of Belief*, California, Hay House, 2008, p. 10–12.

2   Bruce H. Lipton, Ph.D., *Who is in charge in our body? Interview with Bruce in Planeta Magazine* – *Part 2*, [web blog], 7 February 2012, https://www.brucelipton.com/resource/interview/interview-bruce-planeta-magazine-part-2, (accessed 19 May 2017).

3   J. Arthur Rank Organisation, Ltd., from the soundtrack of the film 'Atomic Physics', http://history.aip.org/exhibits/einstein/voice1.htm., 1948, [soundtrack], (accessed 3 December 2016).

4   Rhonda Byrne, 'The Secret', http://www.thesecret.tv/products/the-secret-film-download, 2007–2015, (accessed 23 August 2016).

5   Neale Donald Walsch, *Conversations with God: An uncommon dialogue* – *Book 1*, Sydney, Hodder Headline Australia Pty Limited, 1996, p. 15–16, p. 19.

6   *The Cosmic Giggle*, producers Michael Armstrong and Natasha Murray, United States, 11:11 Films, 2012, [movie].

7   Don Miguel Ruiz with Janet Mills, *The Four Agreements: A Practical Guide to Personal Freedom – A Toltec Wisdom Book*, United States, Amber-Allen Publishing, 1997.

8   Neale Donald Walsch, *Conversations with God: An uncommon dialogue – Book 1,* Sydney, Hodder Headline Australia Pty Limited, 1996, p. 19.

9   HeartMath®, 'Quick Coherence® Technique', https://www.heartmath.com/quick-coherence-technique, (accessed 19 January 2017).

10 Osho, *From Sex To Superconsciousness,* Osho World, 1979, p. 5.

11 *IBID,* p. 19.

12 Don Miguel Ruiz with Janet Mills, *The Four Agreements: A Practical Guide to Personal Freedom – A Toltec Wisdom Book*, United States, Amber-Allen Publishing, 1997.

13 *The Moses Code*, dir. Drew Heriot, writer, James F. Twyman, California, Emissary Productions, 2001, [movie].

14 Office Masaru Emoto, 'What Is the Photograph of Frozen Water Crystals?', http://www.masaru-emoto.net/english/water-crystal.html, 2010, (accessed 6 December 2016).

15 Greg Braden, *Resilience from the Heart – The Power to Thrive in Life's Extremes*, United States, Hay House, Inc, 2014, 2015, p. 4–5.

16 Ancient Egyptian Facts *Ancient Egyptian Facts for Kids*, 'Ancient Egyptian Proverbs', http://www.ancientegyptianfacts.com/ancient-egyptian-proverbs.html, 2017, (accessed 20 May 2017).

[17] Kim McMillen with Alison McMillen, *When I Loved Myself Enough*, Basingstoke and Oxford, Sidgwick & Jackson, an imprint of Pan Macmillan, 2001, pages not numbered.

[18] Kyle Cease Facebook page, https://www.facebook.com/KyleCeasePage/posts/10153329719773062, 2016, (accessed 20 January 2017).

[19] Robin S. Sharma, *The Monk Who Sold His Ferrari,* New York and San Francisco, HarperCollins Publishers Inc., 1999, p. 55.

[20] M. Scott Peck, M.D., *The Road Less Travelled*, London, Rider, 1987, p. 44–45.

[21] John Clarke, Ph.D., 'Corporate Psychopaths', *ABC 'Catalyst'*, 2005, http://www.abc.net.au/catalyst/stories/s1360571.htm, (accessed 5 October 2016).

[22] *IBID.*

[23] 'Marie Curie the Scientist', https://www.mariecurie.org.uk/who/our-history/marie-curie-the-scientist, 2017, (accessed 18 January 2017).

[24] M. Scott Peck, M.D., *The Road Less Travelled*, London, Rider, 1987, p. 45.

[25] 'Jim Carrey and Oprah Winfrey Talk The Power of Intention and Visualization', [online video], 2014, https://www.youtube.com/watch?v=OM2jv-HkcWk, (accessed 15 December 2016).

[26] Richard Carlson, *Stop Thinking Start Living: Discover Lifelong Happiness,* London, HarperCollinsPublishers, 1997, ch. 4.

[27] David diSalvo, 'Breathing and Your Brain: Five Reasons To Grab The Control', *Forbes, Pharma & Healthcare,* 14 May 2013,

http://www.forbes.com/sites/daviddisalvo/2013/05/14/
breathing-and-your-brain-five-reasons-to-grab-the-
controls/#7b98d0b252aa, (accessed 10 September 2016).

28   Harvard Health Publications, Harvard Medical School, 'Relaxation Techniques: Breath Control Helps Quell Errant Stress Response', http://www.health.harvard.edu/mind-and-mood/relaxation-techniques-breath-control-helps-quell-errant-stress-response, (accessed 7 December 2016).

29   Sheila Patel, M.D., 'Breathing for Life: the Mind-Body Healing Benefits of Pranayama', *The Chopra Centre*, http://www.chopra.com/articles/breathing-for-life-the-mind-body-healing-benefits-of-pranayama, (accessed 6 May 2016).

30   David R. Hamilton, Ph.D., 'How a child with Chickenpox stopped itching', *Using Science to Inspire,* [web blog], 5 October 2016, http://drdavidhamilton.com/how-a-child-with-chickenpox-stopped-itching/, (accessed 6 October 2016).

31   *The Moses Code*, dir. Drew Heriot, writer, James F. Twyman, California, Emissary Productions, 2001, [movie].

32   *IBID.*

33   Glennon Doyle Melton, *Love warrior: a memoir*, United States, Flatiron Books, 2016, ch. 14.

34   Rachel Corby, *Rewild Yourself: Becoming Nature*, Stroud, Amanita Forrest Press, 2015, p. 38.

35   Deepak Chopra, M.D., 'Healing Through the 5 Senses', *The Chopra Centre,* http://www.chopra.com/articles/healing-through-the-5-senses#sm.00001gf4jckgoxelvygutqdn0b7er, 2015, (accessed 9 September 2016).

[36] *IBID.*

[37] Rachel Corby, *Rewild Yourself: Becoming Nature*, Stroud, Amanita Forrest Press, 2015, p. 35–36.

[38] Bruce Lipton, Ph.D., 'THINK Beyond Your Genes', https://www.brucelipton.com/newsletter/think-beyond-your-genes-september-2016, 20 September 2016, (accessed 20 September 2016).

[39] M. Scott Peck, M.D., *The Road Less Travelled*, London, Rider, 1987, p. 50–51.

[40] Joseph Campbell with Bill Moyers, *The Power of Myth*, Anchor Books, 1991, p. 100.

A bout the Author

LESLEY MACCULLOCH SPENT TWENTY YEARS LIVING, working, and learning in Australia. She worked in leadership and people management roles before going on to establish her own editing and training business. Now back in central Scotland, Lesley embeds a holistic health and well-being approach into everything she does. Writing is just one of those things.

Follow Lesley at:

Lesley MacCulloch

www.lesleymacculloch.com
https://www.facebook.com/shine.lesleymacculloch

Printed in the United States
By Bookmasters